THE  ACCESSIBLE  CITY

**WILFRED OWEN**

*with the assistance of Inai Bradfield*

# THE ACCESSIBLE CITY

*The Brookings Institution*
*Washington, D.C.*

*Copyright © 1972 by*
THE BROOKINGS INSTITUTION
*1775 Massachusetts Avenue, N.W., Washington, D.C. 20036*

*Library of Congress Cataloging in Publication Data:*
Owen, Wilfred.
  The accessible city.
  Bibliography: p.
  1. Urban transportation.    I. Title.
HE305.O9    388.4    76-39698
ISBN 0-8157-6770-6
ISBN 0-8157-6769-2 (pbk.)

*Title page photograph: United Press International*

9 8 7 6 5 4 3 2 1

THE BROOKINGS INSTITUTION is an independent organization devoted to nonpartisan research, education, and publication in economics, government, foreign policy, and the social sciences generally. Its principal purposes are to aid in the development of sound public policies and to promote public understanding of issues of national importance.

The Institution was founded on December 8, 1927, to merge the activities of the Institute for Government Research, founded in 1916, the Institute of Economics, founded in 1922, and the Robert Brookings Graduate School of Economics and Government, founded in 1924.

The general administration of the Institution is the responsibility of a Board of Trustees charged with maintaining the independence of the staff and fostering the most favorable conditions for creative research and education. The immediate direction of the policies, program, and staff of the Institution is vested in the President, assisted by an advisory committee of the officers and staff.

In publishing a study, the Institution presents it as a competent treatment of a subject worthy of public consideration. The interpretations and conclusions in such publications are those of the author or authors and do not necessarily reflect the views of the other staff members, officers, or trustees of the Brookings Institution.

# Foreword

Concern for the quality of urban life has led to growing disenchantment with the automobile as a major cause of congestion and a primary contributor to environmental pollution. Mounting opposition to cars and expressways has led to increasing support for subways and rapid transit as desirable alternatives.

But the condition of urban transportation cannot be ascribed simply to the methods by which people move. In the view of Wilfred Owen, the author of this study, much of the fault lies in the planless way that cities have been allowed to grow. He argues that what we call the transportation problem is largely the inability to compensate fully for the disorder of the urban environment.

It is central to Mr. Owen's thesis that, if cities were more fit to live in, they would discourage the perpetual motion that is essentially a means of escape. Transportation policies could contribute to this end not only by supplying satisfactory standards of mobility, but by the design and location of transport facilities in support of urban redevelopment and planned suburbanization. This would require at the same time that policies outside the transportation field help create an urban environment in which transportation technology could function. For transport solutions depend partly on the supply of good housing in pleasant neighborhoods convenient to jobs and to community services. The task is to design and build total urban systems that avoid unmanageable transport demands by making the city livable and accessible. This study recommends new institutional arrangements to make transportation an integral part of the process of city building.

Mr. Owen is a senior fellow in Economic Studies at the Brookings Institution. A grant from the Ford Foundation enabled him to observe urban development trends and transportation problems in Europe. Cities in other parts of the world were studied in connection with the earlier Brookings Transport Research Program, financed by the U.S. Agency for International Development, and more recently through a series of economic development missions sponsored by the International Bank for Reconstruction and Development and the Asian Development Bank.

Research on the American urban scene was conducted by Inai Brad-field and Jane Brashares. Principal secretarial tasks were carried out by Louise Richards, Virginia Crum, Margie Barringer, and Margaret Su. Evelyn P. Fisher checked the accuracy of sources and data; the manuscript was edited by Elizabeth H. Cross; and the index was prepared by Joan C. Culver. The author thanks the committee that reviewed the manuscript, and acknowledges the helpful comments of Edwin T. Haefele, Gordon Murray, Joseph A. Pechman, and Robert Sadove.

The views expressed are those of the author and should not be attributed to the Ford Foundation, the Agency for International Development, the World Bank, the Asian Development Bank, or the trustees, officers, and staff of the Brookings Institution.

KERMIT GORDON
*President*

December 1971
Washington, D.C.

# Contents

Tables

# CHAPTER ONE

# The Worldwide Conflict between Cities and Cars

In an age of urbanization and motorization, the way people live and the way they move have become increasingly incompatible. The results, for urban society everywhere, are congestion, pollution, and a growing sense of frustration. Where all-out efforts have been made to accommodate the car, the streets are still congested, commuting is increasingly difficult, urban aesthetics have suffered, and the quality of life has been eroded. In an automotive age, cities have become the negation of communities—a setting for machines instead of people. The automobile has taken over, motorist and nonmotorist alike are caught up in the congestion, and everyone is a victim of the damaging side effects of the conflict between the car and the community. The automobile is an irresistible force that may become an immovable object, and in the process destroy the city.

But the automobile and the highway have also extended man's horizons and opportunities, increased his radius of activity, and afforded him new ways of living and new outlets for leisure and recreation. Cities and their transportation need to be brought into harmony because urbanization and greater freedom of movement both contribute much to the accomplishments of man. Economic and social progress should not be impaired by an unnecessary discord between living and moving. For, as will be shown, the technology of modern transportation is capable of a very different influence on urban life. It can be used to help create the far higher standards of living that rising levels of national wealth in many parts of the world are beginning to make possible. A constructive approach to the application of transportation technology and a broader understanding of the causes of congestion could initiate a new era of city building in which the many other basic problems of urban society would have a better chance of solution.

## The Underlying Causes

Every part of the urbanized world is confronting a fundamental incompatibility between the community and the technology of communications. Cities were first built for security and for the interactions created by people living close together. Since space could be overcome only by foot travel or animal power, distances had to be kept short.

Today there is greater security outside the city than within, and much communication is taken care of electronically. Face-to-face communication is still sought, but the speed and economy of transport make many exchanges possible without the necessity of being close at hand. To maintain communications, nearness has been traded for the ability to overcome distance. However, because highways and automobiles consume space, the attempt to introduce this kind of transportation into cities originally designed with a minimum of space to spare has led either to traffic jams or to methods of alleviating them that have destroyed much of what makes cities worth saving.

Urban areas suffer because the growth of cities and the compression of activities within them have proceeded in conjunction with innovations in transport that have crowded urban areas and spread them thin as well. The resulting volumes of travel have frustrated both the densely packed ancient centers and the newer, disorganized suburbs. The absence of any attempt to reconcile the city and the car has created a conflict between the desire for mobility and the deleterious effects of achieving it.

From another viewpoint, however, cities and automobiles are not in conflict, but are methods of achieving the same human purposes. They both contribute to man's freedom and to his freedom of choice. People who leave the small town or the country for the city gain privacy and options. People who ride in automobiles maintain privacy and freedom and vastly increase their options. The aims are consistent, but indiscriminate use of both systems is leading either to overcrowding or to excessive sprawl—in both cases a communications overkill.

Is it possible to achieve physical compatibility for cities and automobiles to match the compatibility of their communications objectives? Or will present trends lead in the opposite direction toward total victory for one or the other? Will the automobile prevail and the city perish, or will cities muster the political strength to make a stand against the automobile? A preview of ultimate disaster was rehearsed in the summer of 1970 on a global scale. Everywhere monumental traffic congestion and air pollution gave rise to public demands for new engines, cleaner fuels, smaller and safer cars, fewer expressways, and bans on downtown driving. By midsummer the move to banish the world's quarter of a

*Most people who can afford a car have at least one*
Department of Housing and Urban Development

billion motor vehicles from large cities was getting results. Pedestrians took over temporary control of Tokyo's Ginza as air pollution reached critical levels, New York declared Fifth Avenue a pedestrian shopping mall on weekends, and Washington, D.C., cautiously banned the car from its main shopping street one night a week. Cars were banished permanently from selected streets and squares in Rome, Florence, Warsaw, and a dozen other European communities. In the United States legislation was introduced to outlaw the internal combustion engine altogether, and legislation already passed outlaws the exhaust pollution from new motor vehicles as of January 1, 1976. Powerful assaults were also made in Congress against reserving road-user tax funds for building roads. The pressure was on to make part of these funds available for public transit.

But in every part of the world, consumer purchasing patterns seemed strangely inconsistent with campaigns to curb the car. In the United States the previous decade had seen the largest increase in car ownership in the history of the motor age. Both Eastern and Western Europe continued to register record gains in vehicle ownership. In Tokyo consumers went on spending their way into the worst traffic jam on earth. Conditions were no better in Osaka, Nagoya, and other Japanese cities. The world's last major defenses against the automobile fell with the decision of the Soviet Union to push production to a million vehicles a year by 1975, thus ensuring that Moscow traffic would eventually be as bad as it is every place else. In all the world's major cities, from Bogotá to Bangkok to Boston, the conflict between the city and the car is at a point of impending crisis.

### The Motorization of America

The increase in motor vehicle registrations in the United States continues to exceed increases in gross national product, and the automobile explosion has dwarfed the population explosion. In the 1960s the nation gained 23 million people but it also added 31 million motor vehicles. The machine was outstripping the human being. With 1950 as a base, by 1970 gross national product had doubled, motor vehicle registrations had more than doubled, and public transit riding had declined to less than half (see Table 1-1).

The car is a possession that most Americans cherish because it has

TABLE 1-1. *Indexes of Economic Growth and Population, and Transport Trends, United States, 1950–70*

1950 = 100

| Year | Gross national product[a] | Population | Motor vehicle registrations[b] | Transit riders[c] |
|------|------|------|------|------|
| 1950 | 100.0 | 100.0 | 100.0 | 100.0 |
| 1955 | 123.3 | 108.9 | 127.4 | 66.4 |
| 1960 | 137.3 | 118.7 | 150.2 | 54.3 |
| 1965 | 173.9 | 127.8 | 183.7 | 49.1 |
| 1970 | 202.6 | 134.5 | 221.5[d] | 42.8 |

Sources: *Economic Report of the President, February 1971*, pp. 198, 221; U.S. Department of Commerce, Office of Business Economics, *Survey of Current Business*, Vol. 51 (July 1971), p. 13; Automobile Manufacturers Association, *Automobile Facts and Figures*, 1971, p. 18; American Transit Association, *Transit Fact Book*, 1970–71, p. 6.
a. In 1958 dollars.
b. Publicly and privately owned vehicles.
c. Revenue passengers.
d. Preliminary.

given them unparalleled mobility, greater economic opportunities, and a choice of life-styles previously impossible. It is, in the words of Marshall McLuhan, an extension of man, "an article of dress without which we feel uncertain, unclad, and incomplete in the urban compound."[1] Most people who can afford a car have at least one; in 1970, 18.5 million families had two or more.[2] Public transit in the United States, on the other hand, has offered increasingly poor service as the competition of the automobile has caused chronic financial difficulties. The industry has lost more than 10 billion riders since 1950, and patronage in 1970 was less than half what it was in 1925 despite the gains in urban population that have added 100 million potential customers.

In the metropolitan areas of the United States, 80 percent of all work trips are by automobile, and for suburban areas the proportion is 96 percent. Even for home-to-work commuting, much of it to the city center, the automobile characteristically carries 70 to 75 percent of the work force. In central cities of metropolitan areas with more than a million people, there are still more automobile riders than transit riders, the only exceptions being the largest and most densely developed older cities.

1. *Understanding Media: The Extensions of Man* (McGraw-Hill, 1964), p. 217.
2. Automobile Manufacturers Association, *Automobile Facts and Figures*, 1971, p. 47.

The family car is also the principal method of travel from one city to another, generating about 90 percent of all intercity passenger miles in the United States. Public transport has been able to retain as much as 10 percent of the intercity total only because air travel has increased more than tenfold since 1950. Buses, however, have just managed to hold their ground, and rail travel is one-third what it was in 1950 (see Appendix Table A-1).

The way consumers spend their money measures the commitment to the automobile. Food is the major outlay, accounting in 1968 for 23 percent of the total family budget, with housing and household operation the next most important items of expenditure (see Table 1-2). Each of these absorbed some 14 percent of total consumption expenditures. Transportation was the fourth item, commanding almost 13 cents out of every dollar spent, most of it for automobiles. People were spending more for cars than for clothing, and nearly twice as much for transportation services as for medical services.

Table 1-3 shows that, of the amount spent for transportation by consumers in 1970 (excluding business travel), most of it—$72 billion—was for automobiles. Only 7.1 cents of the consumer transportation dollar went for travel by means other than automobile.

Preference for the automobile over public transport has resulted from a variety of physical, financial, and psychological factors. A car is a means of escaping the city, of finding a home where land is less costly,

TABLE 1-2. *Personal Consumption Expenditures in the United States,* *1970*

| Purpose | Expenditures (billions of dollars) | Percent |
|---|---|---|
| Food[a] | 143 | 23.2 |
| Housing | 91 | 14.8 |
| Household operation | 86 | 13.9 |
| Transportation | 78 | 12.6 |
| Clothing and accessories | 62 | 10.1 |
| Medical expenses | 47 | 7.7 |
| Recreation | 39 | 6.3 |
| Personal business | 35 | 5.8 |
| Other | 34 | 5.5 |
| Total | 616 | 100.0 |

Source: U.S. Department of Commerce, Office of Business Economics, *Survey of Current Business,* Vol. 51 (July 1971), p. 24. Calculations and totals are based on unrounded data.
a. Includes tobacco.

TABLE 1-3. *Personal Consumption Expenditures for Transportation in the United States, 1970*

| Purpose | Expenditures (billions of dollars) | | Percent |
|---|---|---|---|
| User-operated transportation | | 72.4 | 92.9 |
| Purchased local transportation | | 2.5 | 3.2 |
| Streetcar and bus | 1.6 | | 2.0 |
| Taxicab | 0.8 | | 1.0 |
| Railway | 0.2 | | 0.2 |
| Purchased intercity transportation | | 3.0 | 3.9 |
| Railway | 0.2 | | 0.2 |
| Bus | 0.4 | | 0.5 |
| Airline | 2.4 | | 3.1 |
| Other | —a | | —a |
| Total | | 77.9 | 100.0 |

Source: As for Table 1-2. Calculations and totals are based on unrounded data.

a. $36 million, which is less than 0.05 percent.

and of expanding the opportunity to find a job. It may be much cheaper to use public transit and taxis than to own a car, but the lower annual bill simply means that people wholly dependent on public transit generally make far fewer trips than does the average car owner. The motorist is encouraged by the nature of his financial commitment to generate more trips. Once he owns a car, he can use it for any given trip at a very low marginal cost. Thus while average total operating cost for a new car is close to 12 cents a mile, direct costs for fuel are 2.5 cents a mile (including taxes).[3] And since no actual cash outlay is necessary for a specific short trip, marginal costs may be considered to be zero, though transit fares may be 25 to 35 cents, or more, each way for a short trip.

From the viewpoint of service provided, the automobile is generally far superior to the bus, since it is always ready to go at the traveler's pleasure, can reach any destination by any route selected, and usually saves a substantial amount of time. It involves less walking, no waiting, and no stopping to pick up and deliver other passengers en route. It is a protection from the rain, the cold, and the heat; it furnishes privacy and guarantees a seat; and for many people it is an important status symbol. And from a practical standpoint, since most city trips are quite short, half of them under a mile, the alternative of using public transit is often out of the question. A good example is food shopping, for which

3. E. M. Cope and C. L. Gauthier, "Cost of Operating an Automobile" (U.S. Department of Transportation, Bureau of Public Roads, 1970; processed).

*The side effects: congestion, frustration, and pollution*
Barry Edmonds/Image, Inc.

the automobile offers the additional advantage of helping to carry the groceries.

Public policy in the United States supports the automotive revolution through extensive outlays on streets and highways. In 1970, public sector expenditures for transportation by all units of government totaled $25.5 billion, or $125 per capita, and over $21.5 billion of this ($105 per capita) went for roads and streets.[4] These outlays reflect the degree of dependence on highways for freight and passenger movement in the United States and the amount of influence public policy has had on how the nation's transportation system has developed. The predominance of motorized movement is obvious from the total bill for freight and passenger movement: out of $188 billion spent for all transportation in 1969, $154 billion was spent for movement on America's roads and streets.[5]

Despite the efforts to accommodate motor vehicles in cities, for millions of Americans commuting by automobile is a headache, and often there is no other suitable choice. The lack of satisfactory service by either car or transit exposes people twice daily to congestion and tension that have come to be an accepted condition of urban living.

The increasingly vexatious problems of moving around in a big city can be judged from the complaints of one resident of New York City. To survive in Manhattan, so goes the advice, make no crosstown trips at lunchtime, no appointments before 11 or after 3, no subway trips except in off-peak hours, and no friendships beyond walking distance.[6] The great advantages of the city, diversity and choice, are being thwarted by immobility and lack of access.

Clearly, today's giant urban concentrations expose people to all kinds of trouble, and transportation is just one of them. The deputy mayor of New York has complained that the city has become unmanageable. Among the ominous happenings in the heat and smog of the average summer are power failures that deny sweltering city dwellers air-condi-

4. Computed from data in Association of American Railroads, "Government Expenditures for Highway, Waterway, and Air Facilities and Private Expenditures for Railroad Facilities" (AAR, May 1971; processed); *The Budget of the United States Government, Fiscal Year 1972;* and population data from U.S. Bureau of the Census and transit information from various sources.

5. Transportation Association of America, *Transportation Facts and Trends*, Eighth Edition (April 1971), pp. 3, 5.

6. Ada Louise Huxtable, "In New York, A Losing Battle," *New York Times* (Dec. 30, 1969), p. 18.

tioning; shortages of water due to ancient pipe systems; a series of transit collisions and breakdowns; rainstorms that transform the subways into storm sewers; near-lethal doses of acrid air, at least half from motor vehicles; monumental traffic tie-ups on the Long Island Expressway; the daily exasperation of stranded railway commuters; and the stack-ups at the airports.

Maintaining a minimum acceptable environment for the big cities of the United States in the last third of the twentieth century is an awesome challenge. The urban future seems destined for overcrowding and loss of amenity just as the demand is rising for enjoyable living conditions made possible by greater affluence and more leisure.

Ironically, New York City's first master plan, which finally appeared in 1969, indicated that the official position favors even higher densities and more upward growth. While the plan acknowledges the problems of jammed highways and subways, the shortage of housing and recreation, and the dirt and pollution of the city, it expresses the belief that concentration is the genius of the city. Only one dissenting member of the Planning Commission viewed the high degree of concentration already attained as unconscionable, and declared further concentration to be "sheer madness."[7]

Meanwhile, New York proceeds to build the tallest structures yet, the World Trade Center's twin 110-floor office buildings in lower Manhattan, with computer-programmed elevator systems to assure the efficient movement of 50,000 employees and 80,000 daily visitors in 190 elevators. The effect of these buildings and other construction projects on transportation outside and on various community services has been left for others to worry about.[8]

### The Dispersal of Urban Living

Big cities, wrote Frank Lloyd Wright, are "vampires" that must die. The universal use of automobiles has made conventional patterns of urban living indefensible.[9] In support of this indictment Bertrand de

7. Karl E. Meyer, "New York Plan Makes Concentration a Virtue," *Washington Post* (Nov. 23, 1969), p. B3.

8. For a benefit-cost analysis evaluating the fifty-story "Inhuman Towers" in mid-Manhattan, see John Fischer, "The Easy Chair," *Harper's Magazine*, Vol. 239 (September 1969), pp. 20, 22.

9. *The Living City* (Horizon Press, 1958), pp. 83–85.

Jouvenel, director of the Futuribles Project in France, brands the densely packed conventional city a product of nineteenth-century thinking, a hangover from the days when we measured distance in miles rather than in minutes. Population statistics indicate that this view is widely held. People with enough money and the right color have reacted to the poor condition of America's cities by joining in a massive out-migration. City dwellers have responded to the motor age much the same as ancient townspeople yielded to the pressures of growth by breaking down the walls. Between 1960 and 1970, metropolitan area growth was almost all in the suburbs—26 percent, but only 5 percent in central cities. In 1970 the suburbs contained 74 million people, 19 million more than in 1960; the central cities contained 62 million, an increase of less than 3 million.[10] And 67 million people lived outside metropolitan areas in small cities and rural areas.

Thus approximately 140 million Americans already live in relatively low-density areas—in the suburbs, in small cities, and in the countryside. Under the influence of the automobile, the giant wave of migration from farm to city has reversed itself and people are pouring back into the country to create new patterns of suburbanization and dispersal. These trends are sustained by the motor vehicle—the car that takes the wage earner to work and the housewife to market; the truck that carries materials to industry and supplies the retail outlets. But they are not being sustained by community plans or by appropriate safeguards to prevent the pollution of the land or to avert the decay of the cities left behind.

It was to be expected that a nation with 70 percent of the population living on 1 percent of the land would be using its 100 million motor vehicles to move out. The city of St. Louis lost 19 percent of its population between 1960 and 1970, while the growth in four adjacent counties ranged from 22 to 75 percent. Michigan's Wayne County—where Detroit is located—lost 1 percent of its population while adjoining Macomb County was getting 53 percent bigger. In the Boston area, the central county lost 70,000 people, but the metropolitan sections of four adjoining counties gained 205,000.[11]

These figures by themselves, however, fail to tell the full story of the

10. U.S. Bureau of the Census, 1970 *Census of Population*, Preliminary Reports PC(P3)-3, United States, "Population of Standard Metropolitan Statistical Areas" (November 1970), p. 10.

11. Ibid., pp. 2, 3, 7.

*The conventional city—genius or madness?*
Department of Housing and Urban Development

*Escape to the suburbs—uncontrolled exploitation of the countryside*
Fairchild Aerial Surveys

exodus from central cities. Nearly all of them were experiencing full flight, and only the surplus of births over deaths among those who remained permitted cities to register a net gain or held down the size of their losses.

The spreading-out process is apt to be underplayed by the official statistics, which show that two-thirds of the population live in 230 urban metropolitan areas. But most of these areas are small, and the large ones are concentrated in relatively few states. There are 31 metropolitan areas with over a million people, but 87 others with fewer than 200,000 people. Moreover, since a majority of those who lived in the largest cities have moved to the suburbs, much of what is called urbanization is not city or big city, but only an urban way of life.

The new low-density living has been strongly supported by transportation. With the availability of air transport, the U.S. center of gravity has shifted westward and southward, and this nationwide loosening-up process has been duplicated regionally by the interstate highway system and the motor vehicle. Transport developments have combined with the telephone, television, and other communications to turn the whole country into one giant metropolis. Today's changing urban patterns reflect the shift from the factory city to the postindustrial society. With the production of goods already secondary to the provision of services, and with a high priority being given to the handling of information and to learning, the new forces generating urban settlements are very different from what they used to be. Along the nation's controlled-access highways a new kind of urbanism is developing. Growing up almost overnight in fields under cultivation only a few years ago are the new research organizations, the modern factory, the regional school, the one-story rambler—often without reference to any visible community. Many of the benefits once derived from close urban association no longer depend on proximity but on the use of the automobile, the telephone, and the airplane. Scale economies have become partly a function of the national economy rather than of urban concentration, and the term "community" for many people has become less a place and more a national or worldwide community of interests. Just "when policy-makers and the world press are discovering the city, 'the age of the city seems to be at an end.' "[12]

But the trouble with spreading out over the countryside is that uncontrolled exploitation of the land is often at the expense of the kind

12. Melvin M. Webber, "The Post-City Age," in *The Conscience of the City, Daedalus,* Vol. 97 (Fall 1968), p. 1093.

of living conditions that people are looking for. Many who drive farther in order to live better find that too many others have had the same idea. The only recourse is to move on again, in much the same way as those who exhausted the soil in an earlier period of history moved on to virgin territory. Sooner or later outward dispersal from one city will run into suburbs spreading from the opposite direction, and the escape routes will be closed. Meanwhile the pollution of the roadsides by unchecked commercial exploitation transforms much of the countryside into the new low-density slums of the motor age.

### `The Worldwide Trend to Cities and Automobiles

The dedication to automobiles once thought to be a purely American aberration is apparently a weakness of the human race. The automobile revolution has already engulfed Western Europe, moved into Eastern Europe, and spread with alarming speed into the totally unprepared cities of the less developed countries. As in the United States, the percentage of the population living in urban areas continues to mount, and the largest metropolitan areas are experiencing the greatest growth. Suburbanization is beginning to accelerate on the American scale in many parts of the world, and traffic congestion is reaching crisis proportions in nearly every major metropolis.

Of the more than 230 million motor vehicles in the world, over half of them are outside the United States. In 1969 there were 78 million vehicles in Europe, 21 million in Asia, 7 million in South America, and 5 million in Africa,[13] and everywhere ownership was concentrated in the cities.

The world balance of motor power has changed almost overnight. Although registrations in the United States increased 42 percent during the sixties, the increase was much greater everywhere else: 130 percent in Europe, 147 percent in Latin America, and 469 percent in Asia. Once the push to motorize got under way, the growth of vehicle ownership occurred very rapidly. The combined fleet of Eastern and Western Europe increased from 12.5 million to 78 million between 1950 and 1969, and Japan's vehicle total rose more than tenfold in the sixties.

There are now twenty-one countries outside the United States that have a million motor vehicles or more. Four of them—France, West

---

13. Unless otherwise noted, automobile statistics in the rest of this chapter are from Automobile Manufacturers Association, *Automobile Facts and Figures*, various issues.

Germany, the United Kingdom, and Japan—have between 13 and 20 million. Several countries are now approaching the intensity of car ownership that has been reached in the United States, which is one vehicle for every 2 persons; among these are Canada and Australia, where there is one vehicle for every 2.7 persons, and New Zealand, with one for every 2.5 persons. Sweden has a ratio of 3.4 persons a vehicle, and the figure for France is 3.7.

Automobile production figures indicate that the upward trend in car ownership will continue to intensify the automotive revolution outside the United States. In 1969, world motor vehicle output was 30 million units, of which almost 20 million were accounted for by other countries. Production in the United States had fallen to 34 percent of the total, from a high of 76 percent as recently as 1950. United States production has either been stationary or declined in recent years, while Italy, Japan, and other countries have registered annual gains of 15 to 25 percent.

The world automotive revolution has been paralleled by the global population explosion. In 1960, urban places having 20,000 people or more accounted for 25 out of every 100 people in the world, as against only 14 out of 100 in 1920. But more important was the trend toward living in very large cities. Everywhere maximum growth has occurred in metropolitan areas, so that concentrations of half a million people or more account for nearly half the world's urban population. The heavy concentration of automobile ownership in these larger, more affluent urban centers has contributed to the rapidly worsening situation in which people live and move.

The great continuums of urban development that extend for hundreds of miles along the east and west coasts of the United States are also a global phenomenon. Giant linear cities have appeared in England, France, Belgium, Holland, Italy, and Japan. These have become unsightly corridors of congestion that make driving increasingly hazardous, inefficient, and unappealing.

### The Crisis in European Traffic

The conflict between automobiles and cities has reached its most acute stage in Western Europe, where there are 65 percent as many vehicles as in the United States, in an area less than half the size. In most European cities it is difficult to drive, to park, to cross the street, or to sleep through the noise. The automobiles that have invaded the historic centers have overrun the sidewalks and turned the great squares into parking lots. Urban life seems to have become centered on the ability to own a car and the ingenuity to find a place to put it.

During the 1960s, the number of motor vehicles in Europe more than doubled. In some countries registrations tripled or quadrupled. The increase was highest for Spain, Yugoslavia, Italy, and the Netherlands (see Table 1-4). In Rome the car has completely taken over the piazzas for parking, intimidated the pedestrian, and made the decibel level intolerable on every major thoroughfare. The sidewalks of many side streets are completely blocked by parked cars. One now encounters colossal traffic jams not only around London, Paris, and Rome, but also in Madrid, Lisbon, Athens, Budapest, and Belgrade. Yet European cities are still far from reaching the peaks of car ownership that rising population and incomes make inevitable.

The situation in Paris is typical of the plight of large European cities that have been flooded with traffic in the postwar period. There are more than 2 million cars in the Paris region; 800,000 enter the city every workday, and 100,000 park illegally. Five out of eight families own a car, and the projection for 1985 indicates a doubling of the number of vehicles in fifteen years, from 2 million to 4 million. In the past five years

TABLE 1-4. *Increase in Motor Vehicle Ownership in European Countries, 1960–69*

*In thousands*

| Country | Motor vehicles | | Increase (percent) |
|---------|------|------|------|
| | 1960 | 1969 | |
| Austria | 530 | 1,236 | 133.2 |
| Belgium | 979 | 2,202 | 124.9 |
| Denmark | 561 | 1,286 | 129.2 |
| Finland | 257 | 753 | 193.0 |
| France | 7,265 | 13,770 | 89.5 |
| West Germany | 5,189 | 14,298 | 175.5 |
| Italy | 2,470 | 9,862 | 299.3 |
| Netherlands | 708 | 2,533 | 257.8 |
| Norway | 301 | 849 | 182.1 |
| Spain | 450 | 2,687 | 497.1 |
| Sweden | 1,331 | 2,350 | 76.6 |
| Switzerland | 573 | 1,389 | 142.4 |
| United Kingdom | 7,179 | 13,405 | 86.7 |
| Yugoslavia | 115 | 705 | 513.0 |

Source: Automobile Manufacturers Association, *Automobile Facts and Figures, 1971,* pp. 26–28.

automobile riding has increased by 35 percent and transit riding has declined 6 percent.

From the results of a 1969 study, Paris officials estimated that the street system could not absorb even a 10 percent increase in peak-hour traffic. On the subway system, rush-hour traffic reduces space to one square yard for each seven riders. The cost of highway and rapid transit deficiencies has become so prohibitive that, according to Paris officials, several thousand dollars in transport investment could be saved for every job moved out of the Paris area.

Affluence seems to lead inevitably to motorization. The proportion of personal expenditures going for automobile transportation increases with rising incomes, and the pattern is the same everywhere. In Belgium in the mid-sixties, transport and communications expenditures were only 3.9 percent of total outlays by wage earners in the lowest-paid categories, but in the top bracket 12.4 percent of family spending was for these purposes, most of it for automobiles. For salaried persons, the range of expenditures for transport and communications increased to an even higher level—17.8 percent—for the highest paid.[14] The British experience with postwar prosperity and motorization has been much the same.

Part of the affluence, it should be pointed out, is the effect of motorization as well as its cause. The automobile has created a vast complex of new industries and services, and a new sense of European community. The economies of France, Italy, Germany, and Britain have been tremendously stimulated by the automotive and related industries. The extent of the economic push is illustrated by France, where production of motor vehicles in fiscal 1969 provided jobs for 10 percent of the French people. Car owners were paying half of all insurance premiums in France, and tax payments by the automotive industry amounted to 16 percent of the national budget.[15]

But a Europe on wheels is moving a long way toward canceling the economic gains from the automobile with the social costs imposed on those who live in cities. The Council of Europe, meeting early in 1970, expressed anxiety over the increasing devastation of the environment and issued a warning against the planless sprawl made possible by the automobile, and the destruction of the cities that would follow unless a strong planning effort redirects the course of urbanization.

14. International Labour Office, *Household Income and Expenditure Statistics*, No. 1, 1950–1964 (Geneva: ILO, 1967), p. 232.
15. *France Actuelle*, Vol. 18 (Nov. 1, 1969), p. 7.

### The Spreading Automotive Invasion

The automobile invasion has moved with great speed into the cities of the developing countries, often resulting in traffic congestion far worse than that in countries with many times the vehicles. Cars are heavily concentrated in big cities having excessive population densities, inadequate street capacity, and resources too limited to permit the heavy investments needed to modernize highways or transit. The strains will increase as times goes on, since developing countries are still in the early stages of motorization and urbanization.

Motor vehicle registrations more than doubled in the nine-year period from 1960 to 1969 in Argentina, Brazil, Chile, Ethiopia, India, Iran, Pakistan, Peru, the Philippines, and Thailand—in Argentina they nearly tripled. National figures of motor vehicle ownership, however spectacular the increase, nevertheless fail to indicate the severity of the traffic crush in major cities. For vehicle ownership is rare in rural areas and villages; it is heavily concentrated in the largest cities, where incomes are relatively high and life-styles often similar to those in other cities of the world. Thus while the entire nation of the Philippines has 83 persons per motor vehicle, the Manila metropolitan area, with a population of approximately 4 million in 1970, had one vehicle for every 24 persons.[16] Manila registrations are increasing at the rate of 20 percent a year, and population is expected to quadruple by the year 2000.

Djakarta in 1970 had 4.5 million inhabitants, and the number is being swelled by 150,000 migrants every year because there are few other cities to which job seekers can move from the poverty of the rural areas and small towns of Java. Djakarta's streets are heavily congested with 100,000 motor vehicles and 100,000 three-wheeled bicycle taxis (*betjaks*). The 1,000 buses now serving the city are unable to handle the traffic, even with average loads double their capacity, and street congestion makes it impractical to operate more buses.[17]

Bangkok has been especially victimized by the automobile. The greater

16. Persons per vehicle in 1969 were 545 in India, 501 in Pakistan, 480 in Nigeria, 126 in Thailand, 39 in Peru, 28 in Brazil, 15 in Venezuela, and 11 in Argentina.

17. "Urban Traffic and Transportation Problems in Djakarta" (paper contributed by the Government of Indonesia for discussion at the Economic Commission for Asia and the Far East, Transport and Communications Committee, Workshop on Urban Traffic and Transportation, Bangkok, December 1970, TRANS/WS/UTT/4 [November 1970; processed]).

Bangkok area now has a population of close to 3 million after a fourfold increase in the past twenty years. In the 1960s, an additional million people required living space. Part of the problem is natural growth (births average about 1,800 a day but there are only 200 deaths), but the major cause of the city's expansion is migrants from rural areas who come there in anticipation of better living conditions. There is no other big city they can go to. The second largest city in Thailand is only one-thirtieth the size of Bangkok.

Into the resulting congestion of urban living in greater Bangkok have been introduced an estimated 300,000 motor vehicles of all kinds, including two-wheelers. The annual increase in registrations is 15 to 20 percent. Approximately 120 new vehicles are added every day.[18] Traffic tie-ups have reached a critical stage, and despite many wide boulevards the street system seems to be operating close to its theoretical design capacity.

In Singapore, 60 new vehicles of some kind are added to the already heavy traffic of that city every day, increasing the total number of vehicles by a quarter of a million in the nine-year period 1960–69. The number of private automobiles also doubled in the sixties, and stood at 130,000 in 1969.[19] This is well over one-fourth the number of cars in Cambridge, Massachusetts, and its adjacent county, or in San Diego County, California. Singapore's dense population, with its heavy pedestrian and bicycle traffic, made the task of accommodating the automoble far more difficult.

In most developing countries the pattern of consumer expenditures for transport show the same high degree of elasticity with rising incomes that is typical of Europe and America. In Rio de Janeiro, consumers in the lowest brackets spend about 3 to 5 percent of their income for transport, while middle-income residents spend 6 to 8 percent and the more affluent 12 to 13 percent. In São Paulo, the highest income groups devote nearly 17 percent of the family budget to transportation. This high rate of spending reflects mostly the purchase and operation of automobiles.

18. J. H. Jones, "Traffic and Transport Problems of Bangkok," in United Nations Economic and Social Council, "Report of the Workshop on Urban Traffic and Transportation, 8–17 December 1970," E/CN.H/TRANS/191 (UN, Jan. 6, 1971; processed), pp. 46–47.

19. Ronald W. W. Loke, "Urban Transportation in Singapore," TRANS/WS/UTT/11 (Economic Commission for Asia and the Far East, Nov. 30, 1970; processed).

But the urban area that overcomes the isolation of the village introduces a new kind of isolation for its low-income residents. They often find it extremely difficult to make the trips between home and place of employment because of the long distances, the congestion of traffic, the crowded buses, and the cost of riding on public carriers. The mixture of mechanized and unmechanized traffic has created intense congestion for all street users. Until recently the use of cars in many cities was confined to business and government and to a few wealthy members of the community. This situation is rapidly giving way to more widespread car ownership and to a partial repetition of the automotive problems plaguing the cities of Europe and North America.

### The Future of the Motor Age

The automobile, notwithstanding its shortcomings, is at the top of the list of what most people want, whoever they are and wherever they live. High taxes and restrictive policies designed to discourage car ownership have not had much effect, nor have the inconveniences of urban traffic. People still drive under the most adverse conditions, or they move out when conditions finally become unbearable.

The automobile revolution abroad puts to rest the idea, long held in the United States, that it was public favoritism combined with the neglect of public transit that led to the motorization of society. It is true that federal, state, and local governments in the United States subsidized the roads and other services that accommodated the automotive revolution. But policies in Europe and other parts of the world were the exact opposite. In most countries abroad, public transit and the railways have received the subsidies, while public policy has been hostile or indifferent to the automobile. Vehicle ownership and operation have been heavily taxed, roads have been poor, parking difficult, and road budgets have only recently begun to reflect the demands imposed by the traffic.

The momentum of the global automotive revolution is impressive, but will it last? Everywhere the conviction has been growing that this particular way of getting around is on the way out. "Strangely, in so progressive an age, when change has become the only constant in our lives, we never ask, 'Is the car here to stay?' The answer, of course, is 'No'. In the electric age, the wheel itself is obsolescent."[20]

20. McLuhan, *Understanding Media*, p. 220.

The automobile is not universally loved. It is, in fact, a prime target of most admirers of the city, many of whom believe that if cars were eliminated the cities could be saved. The automobile is considered the archenemy of the human environment and is referred to by its critics as "a monument to scientific frustration," "a mechanical mistress," and "a dinosaur." The automobile society, according to Lewis Mumford, is the result of one-dimensional thinking, leading to the belief that the principal purpose of existence is not a better life but longer cars to move us greater distances at higher speeds.[21] The car-dominated city is also criticized for creating two separate societies: those who drive and those who are carless. For the millions without cars, many of the economic, social, and cultural advantages of urban living have become meaningless because they are out of reach.

Millions of urban dwellers are the victims of transport technology rather than its beneficiaries. This does not have to be so. Cities were reasonably accessible before the days of improved transportation because they had to be located where they could be supplied, and so grew up at ocean ports and on rivers. They were also accessible within because their size was limited to a population that could be fed and to a radius that could be covered on foot. But mechanization lifted the limits of urban geography, and relatively speaking there are no more transport restraints on how big the city can be, how much space it can absorb, and how much physical chaos it can go on building. There are limits, however, on what can be enjoyed, managed, and tolerated, and in urban America the limits are not far away.

There is no reason to believe that the relentless rate of change in transportation technology during this century will not continue. On the other hand, neither is there any reason to assume that the problems it causes are insoluble. As recently as 1900 there were practically no automobiles in the world, few surfaced roads, no trucks or buses, and no airplanes. In the short space of a few decades the horse and carriage were deposed throughout most of the urban world, along with the ricksha, the pedicycle, the bullock cart, and the camel cart. Old methods have always been thought to be irreplaceable, and man has shown a consistent inability to visualize anything new. But if history has taught us anything, it is that we can expect someday to move faster and more

21. See Wilfred Owen, *Cities in the Motor Age* (Viking, 1959; Cooper Square Publishers, 1970), pp. 90–91.

safely, comfortably, and economically than we do now, by some method that we as yet fail to envision or take seriously. Meanwhile individual transport continues to play the major role, as it has throughout recorded history, evolving from privately owned animals and boats to carts, bicycles, motorcycles, motor scooters, and cars. The stagecoach, the railway, the bus, and the commercial airline have been unable to dislodge the personal vehicle. Whatever the successor to the car, it will have to match many of the conditions satisfied by individualized transportation.

If the age of the automobile is nearing an end, its passing will not be accepted without something better to take its place. In the next few years the automobile itself could become increasingly attractive through measures to achieve greater safety, to eliminate air pollution, and to lower costs through new power sources, longer life, and a reduction in the frequency of model changes. Increasing protection for car occupants could sharply reduce the effects of collisions and lower the cost of insurance, while electronic devices could prevent many accidents in the first place. Automated highways, separation of vehicles from pedestrians, and a variety of improvements in traffic accommodation and control may reduce congestion as well as improve reliability. Other advantages may result from the introduction of smaller cars designed for urban use, from dual-mode systems that make use of guideways on heavily traveled routes and in cities, or from entirely new concepts of mass transit.

# CHAPTER TWO

# The Revival of Public Transport

A nearly universal response to the conflict between cities and cars has been to turn for relief to public transport, to subways in particular. It is not a new solution. In 1900 New York City began planning its subway, following the earlier examples of Boston, London, and Budapest. The purpose was to relieve the spectacular traffic jams created by horses, streetcars, carts, and pedestrians. All of this took place before the automobile had been thought of seriously as a method of transportation, and therefore as a cause of congestion. Now we view the congestion of traffic as the obvious result of the motor vehicle, and look once more to public transport as a way out.

The new emphasis on public transit is justified partly by the lack of space in large cities for unlimited use of the automobile and partly by the demands of people who have no car and depend entirely on public means of conveyance. But even those who do own an automobile may need an alternative when the car is unavailable, so public transportation is a necessary option for many car-owning families.

The necessity for good public transport in cities is dictated first by urban geometry: the number of commuters who can use an urban street system in big cities during peak hours is strictly limited. The limits are set by the proportion of the area devoted to streets, the number of trucks in the traffic stream, the length of the peak-hour period, and the average number of persons riding in each vehicle. A study by R. J. Smeed has attempted to illustrate how the limits operate.[1] The model assumes a two-hour commuter period, 14 percent of city area devoted to streets, an average of 42.5 passengers a bus and 1.45 passengers a car, and 30 percent of the space absorbed by trucks. It also assumes that 85 percent of street capacity is in use, the top practical limit. This reduces average speed to nine miles an hour. On the basis of these assumptions, all commuters in a town center with up to 24,000 jobs could travel to work by car. Beyond this point public transit becomes increasingly necessary. Only 90 percent could drive if there were as many as 30,000 com-

1. "Traffic Studies and Urban Congestion," *Journal of Transport Economics and Policy*, Vol. 2 (January 1968).

TABLE 2-1. *Effect of Number of Commuters on Use of Cars and Buses during Peak Hours*

| Commuters (thousands) | Percentage that can travel by car | Percentage that can travel by bus |
|---|---|---|
| 3 | 100 | 100 |
| 10 | 100 | 100 |
| 30 | 90 | 100 |
| 100 | 49 | 100 |
| 300 | 28 | 100 |
| 1,000 | 16 | 97 |
| 3,000 | 9 | 56 |

Source: Adapted from R. J. Smeed, "Traffic Studies and Urban Congestion," *Journal of Transport Economics and Policy*, Vol. 2 (January 1968), p. 47.

muters, and the proportion falls below 50 percent when the commuter load (under the assumptions cited) reaches 100,000. Table 2-1 gives further details.

Cities also need good public transit to serve those who own no cars for reasons of income, age, health, or choice. Without readily available bus or rail service, these people are often denied equal opportunity for employment, education, health services, and recreation because all such aspects of urban life are inaccessible. In many parts of the world the high-density center city is so far from industrial employment opportunities on the periphery that inadequate means of commuting is a major obstacle to finding a job and keeping it. Even where some form of public transport is available, its high cost and circuitous routing are often insurmountable handicaps to mobility.

The importance of good public transport also lies in its affording commuters a choice rather than exclusive reliance on the automobile. The reasons are suggested by principles of biology and ecology. The simpler a system, the more liable it is to end in calamity. If an agricultural area is planted with only one strain of wheat, a disease to which this strain is particularly susceptible can wipe out the entire crop. A forest that has many types of animals has a better chance of survival than one in which the control of predators is entirely dependent on a single species. Flexibility and options are not possible in simpler systems.[2]

2. Paul R. Ehrlich, "Population," in *Man and His Environment: A View Toward Survival*, Major Background Papers, 13th National Conference of the U.S. National Commission for UNESCO, San Francisco, November 23–25, 1969 (U.S. National Commission, no date), pp. 71–77.

The same principle applies to cities, where it is clear that diversity is an important means of survival. If the job is eliminated, there are other ways to make a living. If the car refuses to start, there should be another way to get to work. If a person is carless, he should not be helpless.

It is also clear that in large cities the automobile is increasingly unable to serve as its numbers continue to expand. The time has arrived when the incompatibility of cities and cars has become so serious that the only solution appears to be a retreat from the automobile in favor of high-capacity, space-saving public transportation. Already one-third of the world's largest metropolitan centers have varying lengths of subways, elevated railways, or surface rail lines on exclusive rights-of-way. Although millions of residents of New York, London, Tokyo, and Paris own cars, a majority of the people in these and other major metropolitan cities rely on public transport, especially for commuting to work in the center city. Altogether a thousand miles of rapid transit lines are in operation, one-fifth of them built since 1945 (see Appendix Table A-2). Several hundred additional miles of subways are under construction or in the planning stage.[3]

### Public Transport in the United States

In the United States the new concern for public transport comes at a time when transit riding has hit the lowest point since early in the century. Transit patronage in 1970 was only 7.3 billion rides, less than half the volume in 1930. Even rapid transit has declined almost 30 percent over the same period, from 2.6 billion riders in 1930 to 1.9 in 1970 (see Table 2-2). Railway commuting has fared no better. Lines that carried some 440 million people in 1930 carry less than half as many today.

Over half of all transit movement takes place in areas with a population of half a million or more. Smaller metropolitan areas with fewer than 50,000 people generate less than 3 percent of public transit rides. The principal patronage is home-to-work travel, and the proportion of commuters using public transportation to the downtown area during peak hours ranges from 50 to 75 percent in Chicago, New York, Philadelphia, Boston, and Cleveland.

3. International Union of Public Transport, *Statistics of Urban Public Transport,* 2d ed. (Brussels: International Union of Public Transport, 1968), pp. 18–54.

TABLE 2-2. *Trends in Methods of Transit in the United States, Selected Years, 1912–70*
*In billions of passengers*

| Year | Streetcar | Rapid transit | Trolley | Bus | Total |
|---|---|---|---|---|---|
| 1912 | 11.2 | 1.0 | — | — | 12.1 |
| 1920 | 13.7 | 1.8 | — | — | 15.5 |
| 1925 | 12.9 | 2.3 | — | 1.5 | 16.7 |
| 1930 | 10.5 | 2.6 | —[a] | 2.5 | 15.6 |
| 1935 | 7.3 | 2.2 | 0.1 | 2.6 | 12.2 |
| 1940 | 5.9 | 2.4 | 0.5 | 4.2 | 13.1 |
| 1945 | 9.4 | 2.7 | 1.2 | 9.9 | 23.3 |
| 1950 | 3.9 | 2.3 | 1.7 | 9.4 | 17.2 |
| 1955 | 1.2 | 1.9 | 1.2 | 7.2 | 11.5 |
| 1960 | 0.5 | 1.8 | 0.7 | 6.4 | 9.4 |
| 1965 | 0.3 | 1.9 | 0.3 | 5.8 | 8.3 |
| 1970[b] | 0.2 | 1.9 | 0.2 | 5.0 | 7.3 |

Source: American Transit Association, *Transit Fact Book*, 1970–71, p. 6. Data for 1912–30 were supplied by the American Transit Association. Because of rounding, figures may not add to totals.
a. Less than 0.05 percent.
b. Preliminary.

The evidence, however, is that transit trends are about to be reversed. The extent of rapid transit construction is impressive. Only minor subway building took place in the United States following World War II, with a total of 16 miles of routes completed from 1945 to 1970. But between 1970 and 1975 some 66 to 76 miles of subway are expected to be finished; for the period 1976–90, another 91 miles are projected.[4] Current programs include the new 98-mile system for the Washington metropolitan area (25 miles in subway) scheduled for completion in 1980 and for first-section operation in 1974. The Bay Area Rapid Transit System in San Francisco is scheduled for operation in the early 1970s. Approximately $8 billion has been committed for modernization and extensions of rapid transit in New York, Boston, Chicago, Cleveland, Philadelphia, and New Jersey.

Other recent transit developments include the New Jersey rapid transit line opened in 1969 between the center of Philadelphia and Camden. In the same year Chicago began operating a rail route in the median strip of the Dan Ryan Expressway. New York City is double-decking

4. Armando M. Lago, "United States Subway Requirements, 1968–1990: Projections and Benefits," *Traffic Quarterly*, Vol. 23 (January 1969), pp. 74, 83.

the Sixty-third Street tunnel for subway commuter trains; Philadelphia is constructing two extensions of the Broad Street subway. Mass transit to serve air travel was initiated by Cleveland's 11-mile transit line that provides 22-minute service to Hopkins Airport, and New York City, as part of a $2.5 billion state bond-financed transit program, is constructing its rail route from downtown Manhattan to Kennedy International Airport, where 20 million travelers move in and out in a single year.

More important than these statistics, however, is the passage of federal legislation to provide $10 billion of aid for public transportation in cities. Under the provisions of the Urban Mass Transportation Assistance Act of 1970, the $10 billion program will be carried out over a twelve-year period, and the secretary of transportation can make contractual obligations for such purposes as the improvement and extension of new rapid transit, the modernization of rail commuter services, and the purchase of buses. A national program for the improvement of local public transport has been undertaken in the United States for the first time in history.

Rail rapid transit systems have usually been built where urban areas exceed a population of one million, where employment in the central business district (CBD) is more than 100,000 people in a concentrated area, and where total CBD trip destinations amount to some 300,000 a square mile. The population density of rapid transit cities is typically in the range of 14,000 to 20,000 persons a square mile with one-way peak volumes exceeding 10,000 to 15,000 persons an hour per corridor. New York City, for example, has over 800,000 persons an hour leaving the nine-square-mile CBD on a weekday evening to provide an average corridor density of 60,000 passengers an hour.[5]

The economy of rapid transit may be enhanced by new technology that reduces the cost of excavation and alters the nature of the transit vehicle and its propulsion. Excavation costs are about one-fourth to one-third of total subway costs, and now run about $5 million per lane-mile under the most favorable conditions. They can be as high as $30 million per lane-mile. It is estimated that if these costs could be reduced to $2.5

5. Herbert S. Levinson and F. Houston Wynn, "Some Aspects of Future Transportation in Urban Areas," *Highway Research Board, Bulletin* 326 (National Academy of Sciences–National Research Council, 1962), p. 30; Wilbur Smith and Associates, *The Potential for Bus Rapid Transit* (Automobile Manufacturers Association, 1970), pp. 4–5, 26–27; John R. Meyer, John F. Kain, and Martin Wohl, *The Urban Transportation Problem* (Harvard University Press, 1966), p. 86.

million per lane-mile, underground transport in densely populated areas would be competitive with surface transport. If tunneling costs were to be reduced to one-tenth of what they are now, there might be 332 miles of subways built in the period 1976–90 instead of the 91 miles now projected.[6]

Relatively few miles of subways will be built, however, compared to the probable new construction of highways, even under optimistic assumptions about cost. Both the costs and the capacity of subways are too high except for major routes in the largest cities. Very few corridors now or in the foreseeable future will generate the amount of traffic that can be moved underground economically. The average cost of $15 million a mile a decade ago (exclusive of right-of-way) has risen to about $20 million a mile. Recently the cost of Washington's projected 98-mile system was estimated to have risen to $30 million a mile. The cost of cut-and-cover construction is somewhat less, since this method, by following the routes of existing streets, avoids or minimizes right-of-way costs. But these savings are partly canceled by losses resulting from congestion while the streets are torn up.

Extensive research efforts are currently being made to develop new concepts of rapid transit and new sources of power. In various stages of conceptualization and experimentation are more than a hundred new transit systems, with such appealing names as the airmobile, aerotrain, tubeflight, hi-line, mini-monorail, monocab, stop-and-go belt, tracked cable car, synchroveyor, transivator, tubeway, urbmobile, and never-stop railway.[7] Some of these efforts attempt to upgrade conventional rapid transit methods for greater speed, comfort, and economy, among them the tracked air cushion vehicle with linear electric motor. Other experiments are directed toward the creation of short-range low-speed vehicles, or people movers, for local distribution and movement within buildings or building clusters. A third set of experiments focuses on the possibility

6. Lago, "United States Subway Requirements," pp. 76, 83; U.S. Department of Transportation, "Third Report on the High Speed Ground Transportation Act of 1965" (1969; processed), p. 38. The importance of research and development in this area is indicated by the fact that an expected 3,000 miles of tunnels are to be built in the United States in the next twenty years. The Department of Transportation estimates that savings of $10 billion might be possible if an adequate research effort were made.

7. Mitre Corporation, "Transportation System Candidates for Urban Applications," Working Paper 7192 (prepared for the Department of Transportation, May 1970; processed).

of finding a technical solution that meets the needs of car drivers and nondrivers alike and furnishes a high-speed service that equals or exceeds the performance of the automobile even in high-density areas. One possibility for accomplishing this without forfeiting the privacy and flexibility of the automobile is the so-called dual-mode transportation network, which combines use of the automobile in low-density areas with an electronic guideway in heavily traveled areas. For those without cars, passenger capsules in the system could be dispatched automatically to selected destinations to provide a kind of horizontal elevator service.

Such a dual-mode, or personal, transit system was simulated for the Boston area to show the effects that might be produced in cities now contemplating new rapid transit.[8] In the mid-sixties, average speed on Boston's transit system was 9 miles an hour and automobiles averaged 16 miles an hour. A third of Boston travelers used transit in the peak hours. It was estimated that by 1975 these speeds would be somewhat improved (to 10 and 21 miles an hour) by planned freeway and conventional rapid transit extensions. The operation of a 400-mile personal transit system (current planning is for 62 route-miles of conventional transit by 1975) was then programmed for the Boston area with substantially better results—a speed-up of both transit and automobile travel to an average of approximately 25 miles an hour, with 38 percent of Bostonians using transit in peak hours as against 32 percent in the 1960s. More important than speed, however, was the opening up of 204,000 suburban job opportunities to low-income families in the central city, who, without cars, could be brought to outlying areas in a half-hour's travel time or less. At the same time, housewives trapped in the suburbs without a second car would have new freedom to move about the metropolitan area.

It was concluded from the simulation in Boston and elsewhere that the benefits of a dual-mode system covering 400 miles would be much greater than those derived from the projected 62-mile conventional public transit system. For most large cities now operating rapid transit, however, the shift to an entirely new system would be more costly than continuing to develop the present network. Also, among cities the size of New Haven, Connecticut, and others with relatively small area and low population density, the cost per passenger-mile of dual-mode systems

8. William F. Hamilton and Dana K. Nance, "Systems Analysis of Urban Transportation," *Scientific American*, Vol. 221 (July 1969), pp. 19–27.

would be about three times higher than in large cities. Large cities not now operating rapid transit and considering the possibility of doing so seem appropriate places to test a dual-mode solution.[9]

### Motorized Transit Potentials

Given the present state of technology, some kind of motorized transport on the surface will continue to be the practical transit solution. The bus now accounts for two-thirds of the passenger trips made by local public carriers in urban areas of the United States but is hampered by street congestion because it shares the streets with automobiles. From one point of view the use of the street system is an advantage, for buses are capable of covering the same ground as cars and of offering the non-motorist the same opportunities of access as are enjoyed by the motorist. But dependence on surface street systems means excessive delays, so that cities are increasingly faced with the need to give bus transit a preferential status or to supply an exclusive right-of-way to convert the bus into a method of rapid transit.

The effort to provide a decongested right-of-way for buses might be achieved through electronic control of street use designed to facilitate bus movement. Buses on limited-access expressways could be given priority and congestion prevented by controlling the number of vehicles allowed to use the system; electronic monitoring of traffic and the use of signal lights would hold traffic below congestion levels and give buses precedence in entering. Motorists excluded from the system would be forced either to use slower surface streets or to drive after the peak period. The cost of ramp construction and control systems and their operation in such cities as Detroit, Pittsburgh, and Houston has been estimated as being between $40,000 and $50,000 a mile, far less than the current estimate of $20 million a mile for new subways.[10]

Experiments are being conducted in a number of large cities, under the sponsorship of state and federal highway agencies, giving motor

9. For discussion of other technological possibilities, see Clark Henderson and others, *Future Urban Transportation Systems: Descriptions, Evaluations, and Programs*, Final Report 1, Prepared for U.S. Department of Housing and Urban Development (Stanford Research Institute, 1968).

10. John F. Kain, testimony in *Economic Analysis and the Efficiency of Government*, Hearings before the Subcommittee on Economy in Government of the Joint Economic Committee, 91 Cong. 2 sess. (1970), pp. 1143–44.

buses preferential use of freeways for express transit. Two reserved bus lanes in the center of a twelve-mile section of Interstate 95 leading into Washington, D.C., save bus riders thirty minutes on the trip into the city. Since the express buses use only a small portion of the capacity of the reserved freeway lanes, there is the possibility of metering other traffic, maintaining speeds above 50 miles an hour, into the bus lanes. The Shirley Highway experiment has reduced automobile traffic in peak hours by 33 percent and increased transit patronage 190 percent. While a modest profit for rush-hour operation is more than offset by losses in off-peak hours, commuters as a whole gain substantially by decongestion of the route and savings in time.

Limiting freeway lanes to the use of buses suggests a broader concept of transportation corridor planning which provides for major routes that can be successively adapted to increased needs as the urban area grows. Initially, the wide right-of-way can be used as an arterial street, with special turnouts for bus stops. The second step is conversion of the corridor to a freeway, with priority given buses entering the traffic stream. Lanes exclusively for buses and other improvements can be introduced if transit volumes require them. Eventually the transition can be made to rail or other guided systems if needed. Meanwhile, in view of the uncertainty about future urban growth trends, reliance on highway-motor-bus solutions for rapid transit should lessen the risk of unforeseen developments, for these facilities, unlike rail subways, can be moved or converted to automobile use if public transit patronage fails to meet expectations. This possibility of hedging with the bus accounts for the reluctance of many American cities to move quickly to construct rail systems.

While a preferential bus system on expressways can help supply suburb-to-city transit and reduce expressway congestion, this is not an answer to the local transit needs of the central city. If surface transport is to be improved in downtown areas, cars may have to be banned from parts of the center city to provide a network of relatively unimpeded bus transit, including service to and from parking facilities surrounding the central area.

An additional possibility for improving public transport is to place greater reliance on taxis or on variations of the taxi that have proved to be effective carriers in other countries. At present, taxis are used mostly by high-income groups because of the high fares—55 to 80 cents for the first mile in most places, and 25 cents a mile thereafter. Nevertheless, low-income users who have no car are increasingly dependent on taxis for shopping and other trips that cannot be made by bus. There is need for a more widespread and less costly system of taxilike transport to meet the requirements of these nonowners of automobiles.

Facts about taxi operations are meager, but the situation in the New York metropolitan area reveals how important a small number of taxis can be and how their effectiveness could be improved. On an average day more than 900,000 people use taxis in New York. Gross revenues are more than half the fare revenues collected from the transit system. Half of all users are professional and managerial workers, and the 2 percent of the people in the area with incomes of $25,000 or more account for 11 percent of the taxi riders.[11]

There are 11,700 licensed taxis in the New York fleet, and four or five thousand "gypsy" cabs that got their start because regular drivers refused to go into the ghetto areas. Taxis travel an average of 100 miles a vehicle in each shift—about 50,000 miles a vehicle annually. Three-fourths of the trips are under two miles, and three-fourths of them carry one passenger. Within half a mile of Fiftieth Street and Fifth Avenue, five times more trips begin by taxi than by private automobile. Cruising accounts for approximately 42 percent of the mileage driven. The large portion of travel by empty cruising taxis indicates the important role that good communications might play in increasing the efficiency of the taxi fleet.

The magnitude of the travel volumes supplied by taxi in New York has been accomplished despite a serious shortage of cabs in the rush hours. Drivers seek to avoid the hours of maximum congestion, and to maintain a taxi monopoly, no new licenses have been issued since 1937. There are 2,000 fewer taxis now than there were then. Licensed cabs were originally issued their licenses, or medallions, for $10, but these have grown in market value to $25,000—a rough indication of how far the supply of taxis falls short of the demand.

In large cities a combined operation of buses and taxis might create a more viable public transit system by the pooling of revenues, the substitution of taxis for buses in low-density areas and off-peak hours, and the provision of taxi feeder service to bus lines. Combining both types of vehicles in one system could conceivably reduce transit deficits by

11. Data from Tri-State Transportation Commission, "Who Rides Taxis," *Regional Profile*, Vol. 1 (February 1969).

matching size of vehicle with volume of business and by providing more door-to-door service.

An effective approach to combining bus and taxi capabilities to fit consumer demand more closely has been developed in large cities of the less developed countries. The hybrid jitney bus, operating under a variety of names, is a small vehicle licensed to provide group riding and door-to-door service by picking up or dropping off passengers on signal. In Manila the 6- and 10-passenger jeepneys are colorfully ornamented vehicles on jeep chassis which operate on fixed routes and supply nearly door-to-door service at reasonable cost. In 1970 there were 28,000 jeepneys in the Philippines and they have greatly reduced reliance on the bus. This has proved a particularly effective way of supplementing the services of the automobile and eliminating the parking problem. Regular taxis also operate in Manila, at about ten times the charge.

Small buses on schedules that respond to rider demand might also offer a service approaching that of the automobile or taxi. In light traffic areas a demand-activated bus system could be made to operate by the use of telephone and computer, and experiments with such a system have indicated potential gains in both economy and service. Telephone calls for service could be logged by computer according to origins and destinations of desired trips. These could be related to the location of buses for selection of the one to be dispatched and the optimal routing to be followed. It is estimated that the system could provide door-to-door transit almost as fast as a private taxi but at one-quarter to one-half the price—only slightly more than conventional bus fare.[12] Operations would probably be most efficient at demand densities of 100 trips per square mile per hour—a level too low for conventional bus service.[13]

### Public Transport in European Cities

Europe provides evidence that an urban population can be reasonably well served by public transportation, that people without cars can be mobile, and that car owners benefit from having an alternative. Surface

12. U.S. Department of Housing and Urban Development, *Tomorrow's Transportation: New Systems for the Urban Future* (1968), pp. 58–59.

13. Ibid., p. 60. A full-scale demonstration, using vehicles and control equipment specifically designed for this purpose, could probably be completed within seven years at a cost of less than $20 million. Pilot projects have been undertaken in Toronto and in Haddonfield, New Jersey.

transport in Europe is moving large numbers of passengers, often with new equipment and usually with good geographic coverage and frequent service. Users of public transportation enjoy attractive bus depots, protected bus stops, good bus and streetcar design, helpful maps, and readily available schedules. Buses and trams are frequently given preferential treatment in allocating street space, low fares have been maintained through subsidies, and lines have been extended to keep pace with urban growth. London, Paris, Rome, and Berlin together have more transit passengers than does the entire United States.

Approximately 190 miles of new rapid transit lines are being built in Western Europe and another 500 miles are being planned. London and Paris have more lines in operation than do all other European cities combined. Their rapid transit systems also include the most extensive subways—99 miles in Paris and 88 miles in London. Moscow has 65 underground miles, and West Berlin, 36 miles. (No other underground system in the world is as large as New York's of 135 miles.) The rest of Europe's rapid transit systems are of relatively modest size. For example, Madrid has 21 miles, Stockholm 14, Barcelona 11, Milan 9, Rome 7, Glasgow 6, and Lisbon 5. All of these are completely underground except Stockholm's system, which is 39 miles long, with about one-third beneath the surface, and Barcelona's, with 95 percent underground.[14]

There are wide variations in the service provided by the subways. Among the new lines, those in Milan, Berlin, and Stockholm are pleasant, clean, and quiet. The Milan system operates steel-wheeled cars that are almost silent compared to the older equipment of London and Paris, although the new rubber-tired equipment in Paris is quietest of all. The Stockholm subway has spacious, well-decorated stations and good equipment. The West Berlin system is also attractive, Rome's clean and uncluttered, and Moscow's ornate though jammed. Much of the new Rotterdam subway is above ground on an elevated structure that detracts from the area. The Lisbon system is clean but noisy, Madrid grossly overcrowded, and Glasgow and Hamburg inadequate in a variety of ways. But it has now been demonstrated that the undesirable qualities of mass transportation in subways can be corrected in the new systems, and overcome to some extent in older systems through new equipment and station renovation.

The latest European transit is the new Regional Express Network in

14. International Union of Public Transport, *Statistics of Urban Public Transport.*

Paris, a high-speed addition to the old Métro, to serve the more distant suburbs. The first east–west section opened in late 1969 runs 13 miles from the eastern end of the city to provide commuters an alternative to congested highways during rush hours. Speed is up to 60 miles an hour, far greater than the old commuter rail route, and 200,000 customers were attracted to the new facility on opening day. Costs were close to $10 million a mile, and the entire rail-subway system will cost $700 million. The one-way fare is 45 cents.[15]

In London only 100,000 people enter the central area by car between 7 and 10 on a typical morning, while a million others use commuter trains, the Underground, or buses.[16] This dependence on public transport occurs even though Londoners own over 2 million cars, and is attributable to the high density of population (27,000 persons a square mile for the whole county), to the physical impossibility of the city's handling any sizable amount of traffic in private cars, and to the high quality of the service.

The high standards of public transportation in European cities reflect generous subsidies, since the cities recognize that the wider benefits to the community cannot be charged to the user alone. The majority of public transport undertakings in Europe operate at a loss, and most cities have arrangements for meeting the deficits. Recently, 53 of 69 transit systems surveyed by the International Union of Public Transport in Europe were found to be operating at a loss that was covered on a regular basis by the state, towns, or municipalities served. In Germany, local transport operations are often merged with municipal utilities— electricity, gas, and water supply—so that the latter can cover the losses on the former. In some cases public authorities guarantee dividends to shareholders. In other cases suburban municipalities make fixed annual contributions to central city transit companies incurring losses (Berne, Lucerne) or cover the deficit on the routes serving their districts (Zurich).

All rapid transit systems lose money. For example, the Stockholm system is owned by a community union consisting of the city of Stockholm and some thirty surrounding municipalities. The union has the power to levy taxes to cover yearly deficits, and it can also support the transit system by making available long-term loans for investment or

15. American Transit Association, *Passenger Transport* (Jan. 2, 1970), p. 3.
16. F. J. Lloyd, "Planning Bus Services in Congested Cities," *Institute of Transport Journal*, Vol. 32 (January 1967), p. 57.

short-term loans for temporary relief. Transit income is about 80 percent of total costs, and fare revenues are less than operating costs. Bus lines have been financially more successful, since they are not obliged to pay the cost of an exclusive right-of-way and the flexibility of the bus makes it possible to adapt to changing patterns of demand. Rapid transit and commuter railways, which are also engaged predominantly in peak-hour movement of workers, suffer from lack of patronage and idle equipment in off-peak hours. The bus has a higher proportion of off-peak use because it can maintain more frequent schedules (having less capacity per unit) and because its frequent stops and greater geographic coverage are better adapted to the needs of shoppers and other off-peak users.

Overall trends in European transit riding continue downward, however, as automobile ownership increases, and during the sixties sharp reductions were experienced in such cities as London, Rome, Berlin, Milan, and Glasgow. A consolidated index of transit patronage in cities of West Germany shows a peak in 1962 and substantial decline thereafter. Taking 1938 as the base period, the index of transit patronage rose from 100 that year to 196 in 1962, with a decline to 164 in 1968.[17]

These overall trends, however, conceal the fact that most of the recent decline has occurred on buses and trams using city streets, while significant gains have been made by subway and other rapid transit lines. Between 1967 and 1969, of fourteen cities outside the United States having rapid transit, twelve experienced an increase in ridership. Only Barcelona and Montreal showed declines (the latter because of the high level of tourist patronage during the Exposition in 1967). But ten cities in the group showed a decline in surface transit (see Appendix Table A-3). In another group of thirteen cities outside the United States served mainly by surface transit, four showed little or no change in ridership and nine registered declines (see Appendix Table A-4). The growing surface congestion caused by expanding automobile ownership is increasing the competitive advantage of subways and other rapid transit on exclusive rights-of-way, while bus travel on streets shared with automobiles is becoming less attractive.

Along with good local transit, Europe has also maintained good intercity and commuter rail services. Government ownership of rail systems and extensive public expenditure programs have made it possible to

17. Data supplied by the International Union of Public Transport, Brussels, February 1970.

provide modern cars and good service. Railway passenger deficits are paid out of general taxes in nearly every country of Western Europe to assure high standards and low fares. Two-thirds of all passengers on the railways of West Germany are being carried at reduced rates for commuters, students, and other special groups. Italian rail passengers fail to cover operating costs, and British railways also suffer large passenger deficits.

The subsidized passenger services of European railways are maintaining high volumes of travel. West Germany's railways carry more than three times as many passengers as do the railways of the United States; the United Kingdom nearly three times as many and France twice as many as in the United States (see Appendix Table A-5).

Where cities are fairly close together, as in Holland, Britain, Switzerland, and northern Italy, the intercity railway provides a kind of urban transit facility. On longer routes, high-speed transport by rail often equals or exceeds the time performance of the airplane, and the scenic attraction of the countryside makes the surface journey especially desirable. Thus the passenger trains, despite direct losses that result from low-fare policies, are substituting for new investment in highways, providing good intercity mobility for people without cars, and offering an attractive additional travel option.

In spite of the good rail and transit service, the congestion of automobile traffic has reached a critical stage almost everywhere in Europe. Whether good transit and especially subways can eliminate automobile traffic jams in cities is highly dubious. Cities with extensive underground systems seem to be more congested than cities with no subways. Rapid transit is essential, but apparently it is not enough. Madrid has very broad avenues, a relatively low ratio of automobile ownership to population, good bus service, and a subway that moves 500 million passengers annually. With all these points in favor of low levels of street congestion, Madrid still suffers severe rush-hour congestion. Traffic on the main avenues is often at a standstill; in the central area, Puerta del Sol, finding space to walk on the sidewalks is frequently difficult; and in the subway it is often hard to find room to stand.

The situation in Madrid indicates that excessive population density and other aspects of urban design adversely affect the circulatory problems of big cities no matter how large the supply of transit. The underlying factor in Madrid is that in a seven-year period during the 1960s a million people moved into the capital, bringing total population to

3 million and population density to 25,000 a square mile, the same as in New York City. Automobile ownership was multiplying at the same time, and the resulting street congestion caused bus patrons to use the subways to avoid the jam. But subway capacity has been unable to take care of the overall growth of demand plus the shift. There are only two big cities in Spain—Madrid and Barcelona—and no effort has been made to encourage growth in other communities. The great waves of migration from farm to city, inundating these two major metropolitan areas, give clear warning that serious traffic jams will be unavoidable in the seventies. Without a dispersal of urban concentration, a head-on clash between cities and cars will be unavoidable.

### Public Transport in the Rest of the World

In spite of the concentration of automobiles in the largest cities of developing countries, most urban travel is accomplished by public transportation. Equipment is generally obsolete and grossly overcrowded, and those who have the money to ride are subject to many discomforts and inconveniences. As in the United States, the home-to-work journey for low-income workers is especially difficult, since many of the most attractive jobs are far from the central city slums. For a variety of reasons, therefore, most big cities are now beginning to plan for rapid transit as a means of coping with increasingly bad conditions.

Caracas, Bangkok, Manila, Singapore, Hong Kong, and other cities are approaching the stage where relying on motorized transport using inadequate streets is futile. For these cities high population density and rapidly growing numbers of cars mean that mass transit on the surface is rapidly deteriorating. Some type of rapid transit on an exclusive right-of-way seems essential if the big city is to continue to function.

Latin American nations are experiencing a boom in subway building that may involve billions of dollars during the next decade. The Argentine government is planning major renovation and extension of the 20-mile Buenos Aires subway, which carries 242 million passengers a year. Mexico City opened its subway in 1969, when the first segment of the planned 26-mile system began operating. The rubber-tired, French-built trains average 20 miles an hour, serve forty-nine stations, carry a quarter of a million people a day, and make the run from one end to the other in less than half the time it takes to go by automobile in typical traffic. Santiago, Chile, is completing a 35-mile system combining subways with elevated and surface rail systems. In Brazil, both Rio de Janeiro and São Paulo are building new subways.

While low-income families in all countries need adequate public transport, the key question, as in the United States, is whether a limited system of rapid transit or surface transit by bus and taxi is the answer. The high cost of rapid transit and its drain on municipal finances even in affluent societies suggest that it may not be a practical solution where per capita incomes are low and many other needs, housing in particular, are pressing. These other needs will have diminishing chance of being met if excessive resources are allocated to transport. Moreover, while increasing numbers of cars create pressure for an underground system, the subway may not relieve conditions on the surface but merely shift some public transport riders from bus to rail. The majority of transit riders will probably continue to use surface buses, and without restrictions on automobiles, they will still be subject to the congestion of automobile traffic.

The nature of this dilemma is illustrated by the case of Caracas. The city is confronted by severe congestion as a result of population gains and automobile ownership and is planning a rapid transit system to alleviate the situation. Caracas has a population density three times that of Washington, D.C., and with 200,000 automobiles, the travel of Caracas residents is about equally divided between cars and transit. It has been concluded that a subway will have to be built to help overcome the crippling congestion that further car ownership and increases in population make certain in the immediate future.

But the estimated effects of the subway on travel in Caracas do not provide an impressive long-term outlook. With the doubling of the city's population, total trips are expected to increase from 2.5 million to 6.4 million a day, half by public transit and half by automobile. Most of the subway passengers will still rely partly on transfers to bus or jitney taxi, so that transit passengers using surface streets will number 2 million more than today. These riders will have to contend with more than three times as many private cars as there are now, which means that, while the subway will accommodate more travel, congestion will be worse than ever.

This impasse is compounded by the fact that 25 percent of Caracas's population are squatters living in unsanitary hovels, and their number is expected to double during the next twenty-five years to a total of

*The bus must compete for street space*

*Congestion is not necessarily eliminated by rapid transit*
Massachusetts Bay Transportation Authority

800,000. It is questionable whether so large a segment of the city can be expected to subsist in the midst of what by that time should be substantial affluence. Should extensive investments be devoted to transportation when there is so great a need for housing and related community facilities?

In Hong Kong the problem is much the same. The half-million daily trips made by all forms of transport in 1965 are expected to increase to five times that number by 1986. If a new rapid transit system is in operation by that time, automobile trips are still expected to be four times the 1965 volume. This has led to the suggestion that along with the subway a high tax to discourage the use of private cars would be necessary. Even with a substantial tax increase, car ownership is expected to double by 1986, but the number of cars using the streets during rush hours might be cut in half by user charges reflecting high peak-hour costs.[18]

The implication of these figures is that even with subways taking some of the load, traffic may be intensified unless the movement of private cars is restricted by regulation or higher user charges. If the banning of automobiles on designated streets or in congested areas were accepted, the preferable mass transportation solution might be to use the vacated streets for better public service, thus avoiding large capital outlays on subways that are only a partial solution.

The desirability of spending for housing and sanitation rather than for subways is highlighted by conditions in Bombay. The metropolitan area, with approximately five million people, has few cars and a public transport system that is already extensive. The suburban railways carry two million people every day—30 percent of all passengers carried by the Indian Railways. Many commuters are forced to ride on the roof or hang from the windows, and the frustration and resentment of riders periodically finds expression in setting fire to the railways. The additional two million commuters who travel by bus are subject to comparable indignities. Ancient and overloaded buses break down nearly three thousand times a month, and traffic congestion on overloaded highways reduces average speed to less than four miles an hour on some routes.[19] Now the remedy being proposed is a subway system.

The Bombay situation illustrates, in an exaggerated way, the mistake

18. "Road and Rail Plans for Hong Kong," *Road International* (March 1969), p. 27.

19. Wilbur Smith and Associates, *Bombay Traffic and Transportation Study*, Vol. 1 (1963), pp. 59, 73.

of attempting to accommodate congestion rather than dealing with the underlying factors that generate it. Population density of 115,000 persons a square mile in the central area make the daily crush inevitable, whatever the method of transport. While further transport solutions might temporarily alleviate the problems of moving that result from overcrowding, these are not the major problems of Bombay. The most urgent needs are for housing, schools, water, sanitation, and amenities of all kinds. Seventy-five percent of the population live in rooms housing five to ten people each, only 15 percent of the dwellings have a toilet, and only 28 percent have water. There is not even sufficient space under the streets for the extra sewage facilities needed. One out of every five persons uses the sidewalks to cook, eat, and sleep.[20] Providing more transportation capacity promises to worsen congestion rather than diminish it.

There is growing evidence that rapid transit may be no more successful than express highways in satisfactorily solving traffic congestion when conditions of high density are uncontrolled. Japan provides a lesson for other Asian countries. Tokyo has taken nearly every conceivable means of improving mass transportation. There are about 100 miles of subways, a monorail, and a large network of public and private railways. Yet a government White Paper has now concluded that the effort to accommodate more people in the Tokyo metropolitan area must be resisted and that instead steps must be taken to create population centers outside the present congested area. Good mass transportation in Tokyo made overcrowding possible, but rising incomes and the demand for a higher quality of urban life have made the result increasingly intolerable. Japan expects to extend the area of urbanization and to reduce densities by continuing to expand Tokyo's rapid transit system and at the same time building 5,000 kilometers of high-speed rail line throughout the country to serve a more dispersed network of cities.

### Automobiles and Transit: The Failure to Collaborate

Clearly, the fortunes of both the automobile and public transport are interdependent. The success of each depends on what is done about the other. Yet in nearly every city in the world these two major parts

20. Data from a paper by F. P. Antia, "Any Hope for the Slum City?" (Bombay).

of the single problem of how to provide adequate mobility for the urban population are being separately planned and financed. The outcome is reflected in the severity of street congestion, the absence of acceptable standards of public transport, the lack of genuine travel options, and the neglected travel needs of large segments of the population. The continuing rise in car ownership and the growing obstacles to providing satisfactory public transport point to the need for a combined strategy.

Highways and streets and their operation affect the fortunes of both the automobile and transit. Parking is a transit problem as well as an automobile problem, because transit riders are delayed by congestion that results from parking. The improvement of transit and attendant increases in patronage also help automobile movement by releasing street space for driving.

If transit ridership is to be maintained, the quality of equipment and the frequency and geographic coverage of the service will have to be greatly improved in most cities and much more money spent for this purpose. For public transport systems to be self-supporting to any substantial degree, however, fares, already high in many cities, would have to go still higher. Since most nonowners of cars are in the lower income brackets, the high cost of riding would curtail mobility or be a serious financial burden. For car owners, increased fares would mean further diversion from transit to driving.

Rising fares may be expected to have the undesirable effect of increasing traffic congestion for everybody. Part of the reduction in transit patronage following a fare increase is attributable to the decision of riders to use their automobiles. This is particularly the case where more than one member of the family commutes. For while an extra passenger using the bus pays an extra fare, an additional passenger in the family car costs nothing. The best chance of encouraging the use of public transport is, therefore, good service at the lowest possible charge, combined with measures to ensure that automobile travel pays its way.

The advantages of having thirty or forty people ride in one public vehicle instead of in, perhaps, twenty-five private cars are considerable whenever traffic reaches volumes anywhere near the point of congestion. A study made in Great Britain shows that when traffic is light the time taken to travel a mile in town centers is about 2.6 minutes. As traffic becomes heavier, however, there is a continuing rise in trip time, and when traffic volume equals as much as 75 percent of street capacity, any increase in this volume results in a sharp increase in congestion. For example, at this point it takes only a 24 percent increase in traffic to produce an 89 percent increase in trip time.[21]

Much can be gained, therefore, by reducing the amount of movement by car and by maintaining total traffic well below the theoretical design capacities of city streets. Pricing road services to reflect social costs might help prevent city streets and expressways from becoming overloaded. Such pricing might act as a rationing device, diverting to transit those motorists unwilling to pay the price. Another approach is to subsidize transit to a greater degree to reflect its social benefits or cost savings to the community. By keeping fares low or eliminating them altogether, it might be possible to minimize both the total passenger transportation bill and the level of congestion.

Congested metropolitan areas have reached a point where immediate relief could be obtained for both the motorist and the transit rider by a thorough revision of financial policies and pricing methods governing public and private transportation. The automobile appears to be paying in user charges the total cost of streets and highways, although the revenues collected are not being allocated in sufficient amounts to the cities where the costs are incurred. Automobiles are not covering the cost of parking, however, much of which is provided on the streets without charge or at subsidized parking-meter rates. Nor are they paying for the effects of pollution, environmental destruction, and other social costs. An additional factor influencing automobile-transit competition is that user charges are uniform regardless of where and when the travel is performed, so that peak-hour automobile commuters are being subsidized by off-peak drivers.[22]

Much of the capacity of new urban highways was built primarily to take care of traffic in the peak. If incremental costs of peak-hour traffic were only 20 percent more than those of off-peak traffic, the 40 percent of driving that is home-to-work travel would cost 50 percent more than is now being paid. If highway costs should be as much as doubled by peak-hour traffic, peak users ought to be paying three and a half times what they pay now.

21. Smeed, "Traffic Studies and Urban Congestion," p. 41. Smeed's findings make a strong case for charging more for automobile use in peak hours and subsidizing buses with these revenues.

22. For a fuller discussion of automobile and transit subsidies and user charges, see Wilfred Owen, *The Metropolitan Transportation Problem* (Brookings Institution, 1966), pp. 142–64.

The social costs not covered by motor vehicle taxes include air pollution, accidents, and the noise, nuisance, and undesirable aesthetic effects of congested streets and parking. Damage to property from air pollution in the United States, for example, is estimated at $11 billion a year, and 60 percent of this cost is attributed to motor vehicles. This means that $6.6 billion in pollution costs should be charged against drivers. Accident costs not covered by insurance amount to $6.5 billion. Thus measurable social costs not being paid by U.S. motorists total more than $13 billion annually. With 100 million vehicles in use, recovering these costs would increase user taxes by about $130 a vehicle. Additional charges would be justified to cover unknown health hazards from air pollution, the effects of noise, and the environmental deterioration brought on by parked cars and clogged streets.

The extent to which a social surtax or peak-hour charge would in the long run affect the volume of driving is not known. If social costs were charged to users, manufacturers could compensate for them by designing vehicles to achieve more operating economy or by avoiding annual model changes. The industry might also reduce the social costs themselves by making the necessary changes in power plants and fuel, and by engineering the car to diminish accidents and to protect occupants from physical damage when accidents do occur. These possibilities suggest that an appreciable reduction in the use of the automobile would probably not result from a general increase in motor vehicle taxes; that a more direct method of coping with social costs would be to specify vehicle performance or ban the car from areas in which it is a nuisance.

Payment for parking is in any event a more important element in the cost of urban automobile use, and might be a more practical way to arrive at an equitable pricing policy. Many motorists use free parking space provided by their employers. Free or subsidized parking in the company garage or parking lot is a fringe benefit in lieu of salary that favors automobile owners over nonowners. The amount of subsidy often exceeds what nondriving employees pay to ride the bus. From a public policy viewpoint, it might be preferable for companies to subsidize workers who use transit by issuing free passes as a fringe benefit.

For automobile users who do not receive a parking bonus where they work, parking on the street may confer a municipal bonus. How much this amounts to can be judged by the difference between the parking charge at the curb and the charge for parking in an adjacent lot. If curb parking is permitted without charge and parking in an adjacent lot or garage is $2 a day, the public subsidy for 250 working days a year for a million drivers is about $500 million. If 10 million of the 100 million vehicles in the United States receive such benefits, their annual subsidy comes to $5 billion—three times the annual fare revenues collected from U.S. transit users. The remedy is to ban street parking, charge its full cost, or provide compensatory subsidy to public transport.

In high-density urban centers, an effective decongestant might be to eliminate street parking and as a substitute offer good local circulation from fringe parking areas by minibus or other secondary distribution systems. If parking bans proved politically unfeasible, the goal of achieving fair competition between automobile and transit might be accomplished by matching automobile parking subsidies with comparable financial assistance to those who ride transit. There is a good case for using motor vehicle tax revenues to supply public transit without charge, since this would encourage a shift from automobile to transit and decongest the streets for everybody.

The D.C. Transit System in Washington has estimated that a subsidy of $37 million a year—less than the cost of running the police department—would make it possible to maintain present schedules and carry everybody free, with a balance left over for profit.[23] Free transit for the nation's capital might be a good place to start, since a demonstration project is needed and the city is at a point where the decision must be made either to continue private ownership or to purchase the system for public operation. Requiring exact-fare collection on the buses has also introduced inconveniences that suggest eliminating fares altogether as a logical next step.

For many cities a no-fare bus system, if accompanied by improvement in service, might increase public transportation patronage and satisfy total urban transport requirements at far less cost than alternative investment in rail rapid transit. Free bus service would also be more responsive to the travel patterns of low-income families in central cities who need a dense network and frequent service.

The total amount now spent for transit by consumers in the United States is $1.6 billion a year. If fares were eliminated and service improved, both to accommodate a greater number of people and of routes and to do so with better equipment and more frequent service, the cost

---

23. London Transport, for instance, has estimated the cost of eliminating transit fares in that city at $170 million to $200 million annually.

would be increased substantially—to perhaps two or three times the current expense. But savings in automobile operating costs and a reduction in the number of families now requiring two or more cars (there are nearly 18.5 million multiple-car-owning households) might more than compensate for the added transit outlays. The principal aims, however, would be to reduce street congestion and parking problems, provide a sastifactory transportation option, and supply access to the city for the nonmotorist.

## The Transit Dilemma

As the upward trend in automobile ownership continues, cities all over the world face the common problem of how to maintain essential public transportation. The effort is thwarted in the first place by the automobile's competition for street space, which reduces the efficiency of surface transit and increases its cost. Going underground or providing an exclusive right-of-way for transit eliminates this interference but is very costly and is limited to a relatively few miles. If higher transit costs are reflected in fares, the result is likely to drive people away from transit. And as affluence increases the proportion of the urban population owning automobiles, even good transit service is often spurned in favor of using the private car, especially as the nature of urban trips is altered by the changing locations of work and home.

There is also a question whether conventional rapid transit can serve the travel patterns of low-income riders. Rapid transit does not provide the means of making short trips for shopping and other local daily needs, and it is expensive. Nor will it provide satisfactory transportation to employment on the fringes because of the physical impossibility of covering the extensive suburban areas that offer potential employment. Suburban residents who use rapid transit into the city can do so because an automobile gets them to and from the outlying station.

Rapid transit solutions may also create congestion rather than alleviate it. For while some routes may never develop sufficient traffic to warrant a subway, the high-density routes that do require such facilities may encourage areas of high-density growth that generate more transit traffic than can be conveniently handled without lowering service standards. Without effective land-use controls, the tendency toward greater concentration of economic activity will make congestion, including street congestion, worse than ever. This phenomenon, as noted earlier, is projected for many cities planning rapid transit systems. After the Washington subway has been completed, for example, it is anticipated that 1990 travel by automobile, rather than diminishing, may be more than double what it was in 1960.

The concentration of new building construction following the introduction of rapid transit can have the advantage of balancing the vertical transportation in buildings with the high capacity of horizontal transportation in subways. But without adequate controls it can also lead to a new imbalance (at higher volumes) by creating more traffic generators than can be accommodated. Thus the goal of maintaining a reasonably close relation between new rapid transport capacity and the resulting urban concentration may require restrictions on automobile driving, avoidance of uncontrolled building, and the design of buildings and neighborhoods to create a better balance between residential and work space. Otherwise multibillion-dollar transit investments may in the end produce traffic conditions no less burdensome than the conditions they were intended to correct.

The root of the problem is that location decisions are based on the economic feasibility of individual structures, and not on the total costs incurred by the community. A building constructed on a new subway line can be a sound investment for the owner, while a series of such investments may create so many demands on municipal services that collectively they prove to be an economic disaster. This is why a community design establishing the densities and locations of urban activity and relating them to whatever transportation capacity will be available is necessary. Without public control over how urban land is to be used, transportation needs are likely to be miscalculated, both for automobiles and for transit. Urban congestion cannot be cured simply by supplying more transportation; the solution lies in balancing the supply of transportation and the demands created by the physical characteristics of the city and in governing the ways growth occurs.

Is the attainment of such a balance actually feasible? Can transportation be developed as a subsystem of the larger urban system? The global laboratory of cities reveals that a great variety of attempts are being made to accomplish this result, both in large-scale urban redevelopment projects and in new communities planned not only to provide mobility, but to ensure accessibility as well.

# CHAPTER THREE

# Urban Goals and Community Design

Whatever the prospects for containing the automobile in urban areas or moving with greater ease by public transport, neither effort by itself will get to the heart of the problems suffered by most of the world's cities. They are victimized not only by traffic congestion, but also by a mixture of severe economic and social problems that stem to a large degree from the chaotic way cities have been allowed to grow. Greater efforts in the transport sector often serve only to sustain ways of urban life that have become unbearable.

The trouble with much of the urban transport effort is that the improvements being made either help to crowd more people into inadequate space or encourage a kind of spread-out city that denies people the satisfactions of being part of a community. Both have resulted in environmental deterioration and in the neglect of housing and infrastructure and services. As urban population and congestion continue to grow, the primary concern of public policy should be not simply to move traffic but to create the conditions that will lead to a satisfying urban environment. Current transportation policies are doing just the opposite: rapid transit is reinforcing the move toward the unmanageable metropolis, and measures to accommodate the automobile are hastening the dissolution of community.

## The Accidental City

The basic difficulty of urban growth all over the world is that decisions about the use of urban land are being made by a host of private parties without the guidance of comprehensive plans or community goals. The result is heavy social costs, which include the high costs of a bad environment and large outlays for transportation and other services needed to cope with the outcome. Transportation technology is supporting a wide variety of undesirable cities and shoddy suburbs. The only remedy is to recognize that anything is technically possible and to choose the kind of environment to be sought. The laissez-faire city is likely to end in disaster.

Many of the world's big cities are already approaching that fate as they become more crowded, polluted, and disorganized. Transportation succeeds in keeping things moving, but in the process it is largely responsible for the depressing and ugly environment, the pollution of the air and the land, and the destruction of amenities that contribute to good living. Transportation must be viewed in a new light, not simply in terms of mobility but in terms of a better city.

What kinds of urban futures are possible, and what are the goals we should seek? Obviously, many will prefer the big city, others the country, and throughout the life cycle people will change their minds about how and where to live. In the whole range of urban futures transportation technology will be able to serve effectively only if it is furnished as part of a total development strategy. This is what is lacking, and why both large cities and small and their suburban surroundings often fail to create an acceptable home for human beings. The great metropolitan city and the low-density suburb will both be wanted and will both be possible. The task is to see that both are designed well instead of poorly, and that the transportation that makes them possible also makes them desirable.

The great frustration today, we are told, is that people have become passive consumers of whatever technology offers rather than pioneers of the new standards of living that technology makes possible. Cities are being built and rebuilt "not with human purposes in mind but with technological means at hand."[1] The human purposes are adequate food and shelter, education, health facilities, good public services, and amenities of all kinds. How these needs are met, however, depends to an important degree on how transportation is provided. Transportation policies can help create new and satisfying urban settlements or they can destroy the chance of achieving an acceptable environment. Instead of being used to battle the existing congestion, transportation should be used to guide new growth into redeveloped areas and new cities built to serve community goals. Technology makes a wide range of choices possible, but the choices must be made. The question for public policy makers is how the ability to move freely within the city and in or out of it can serve to make urban goals easier to attain. This is not the same as the familiar preoccupation with getting the largest number of people

1. Archibald MacLeish, "The Great American Frustration," *Saturday Review* (July 13, 1968), p. 14.

moved between two points at the lowest possible cost. Transportation is the means by which a whole city functions and human aspirations are furthered. The freedom to move will determine whether or not it will be possible to participate in the activity and diversity of the city.

The United States aired its urban problems and articulated its goals many years ago in a report made for the President.[2] Then, as now, the problems were slums, poverty, poor housing, air pollution, lack of adequate education, and others equally familiar. Emphasis was on the need for a national view of urbanization—to delineate the areas to be preserved for recreation and natural beauty and to identify the areas in which urban development should be encouraged. Special concern was expressed about the poor condition of housing and the persistence of unemployment and inadequate incomes. Although rising incomes have moved many families out of the poverty class since then, approximately 26 million Americans still have incomes below the amount considered necessary for minimum standards of living, and all of the problems of inadequate cities that were with us then are with us still.

Nearly twenty-five years later, the President's Commission on National Goals said the same things all over again.[3] Corrective action was called for to eradicate the slums, eliminate the process of decay in the larger cities, avoid the compulsory concentration of low-income and minority groups in the old central cities, and overcome haphazard suburban growth. And still there has been no substantial progress toward alleviating the problems of urban living. Heavy demands have been made on transportation to compensate for planless communities.

Emphasis on highways and automobiles has helped make it possible to get from one place to another faster, but meanwhile the space between places has become greater, the relationships among urban activities more complex, and the environment more repellent. The domination of traffic, the random location of economic activities, the absence of amenities, and the dual urban society represented by the affluent suburbs and decaying centers have created a kind of urban treadmill. We are in a constant state of motion without making much forward progress.

In essence, since no one is responsible for creating whole cities, trans-

2. *Our Cities: Their Role in the National Economy,* Report of the Urbanism Committee to the National Resources Committee (Government Printing Office, 1937).

3. *Goals for Americans,* Report of the President's Commission on National Goals, Administered by the American Assembly, Columbia University (Prentice-Hall, 1960), p. 13.

portation is called on to make the disorder viable. What is needed is a way to combine transport with other urban programs, to influence the demand for movement, and to substitute proximity for propulsion. The goals of better housing, access to jobs and recreation, and other community improvements should be the guidelines for transportation policy.

There is a general pessimism, however, that nothing substantial can be done about the condition of existing cities and the accomplishment of something better. According to the common notion, since ugly urban concentrations are already with us and represent a tremendous capital investment, making any radical changes would take too much money and too much time. But actually cities are living organisms in a constant state of rebuilding, and the opportunity to begin creating a more satisfactory human environment is offered every day. Each year the United States builds new urban structures equal to a new Philadelphia. Every month's construction adds the equivalent of Toledo, Ohio. Between now and the end of the century, the United States will be doubling the area of the country devoted to urban living, and half the population will be living in houses that do not exist today, on land that is now woods and fields. In the developing countries, by the end of the century there will be 1,400 million more urban residents who will have to be accommodated one way or another.[4] We are continually building the very things we say are not possible, but doing so in a haphazard way. We could, if we wished, be directing urban forces toward the kinds of communities we want.

In Britain at the turn of the century, Ebenezer Howard proposed that the public acquire land on which private industry could erect the social city, for rich and poor, with access provided by the new technology of transport.[5] Experiments with the idea have met with varying degrees of success in urban redevelopments and planned cities throughout the world. Transport and communications have vastly expanded the possibilities that a new kind of urban region can provide the basis for reconciliation between the automobile and the city, between transportation and housing, and among income groups and races. This would be the accessible city in the total sense, and its design principles would apply to the restoration of old cities as well as to the creation of new.

4. United Nations, Department of Economic and Social Affairs, *Growth of the World's Urban and Rural Population, 1920–2000* (UN, 1969), p. 71.

5. *Tomorrow: A Peaceful Path to Real Reform* (London: Sonnenschein, 1898), reissued as *Garden Cities of To-Morrow* (London: Swan, Sonnenschein, 1902), chapter on "Social Cities."

Generating much concern over urban transportation problems as such is difficult because there are too many other problems that cry out for attention. In fact, the single-purpose quest for ways to speed up traffic is often a frivolous use of public funds. But transportation programs that help solve problems of housing, public services, and the environment take on a new significance. Rather than merely supporting cities that nobody wants to live in, these transport efforts can help create the cities people want.

Every nation lacks adequate housing, and a solution may prove to be one of the most important instruments for achieving economic development and social progress. But an obstacle that has assumed major proportions in the past several years is the high cost of land and the lack of sites on which to build. In the old central cities, assembling the required land is difficult, and in suburbia the new developments do not offer a range of housing prices, acceptance of minorities, or an adequate economic base to exercise a check on commuter congestion.

These problems can be solved in two ways. One is redesigning the old cities, to make way for "the new city in city." The other lies in guiding urban growth through a combination of new highway and transit investments plus public land acquisition to help bring about an orderly urbanization process in place of the urbanism that is accidental, divisive, and designed for profit instead of for people. Planning a nation's economic growth should be accompanied by planning for its spatial growth.

The necessity for planned urban development based on community goals is not diminished by prosperity. Higher levels of gross national product have not automatically alleviated the misery in the center cities. The slums have been virtually untouched by affluence, and often the effect of the past decade of rising national incomes has been to make conditions in the cities worse. Mass transit and expressway programs are not going to do much to relieve the problems of the suburbs and cities unless they are made part of a broader program for housing, reconstruction, and planning for future growth. The nontransportation aspects of urban development will be just as important as what is done to improve the ways people move. The single-purpose, least-cost solution aimed at moving traffic will have to be abandoned in favor of creating an environment in which adequate shelter and decent neighborhoods are convenient to job opportunities, recreation, and all that urbanization, in theory, has to offer. Plans for transportation must shift the emphasis from coping with congestion to encouraging communities without congestion.

*Boston—"new city in city"*
Aerial Photos of New England

Transportation, it is pointed out, is a means to an end, but in the age of automobiles it has become an end in itself, often to the detriment of other values. The fact lost sight of is that the potential of transportation for furthering community purposes is as great as its potential for community destruction. The ways in which it can help are demonstrated in efforts throughout the world to rebuild existing cities and to build entirely new ones.

### Accessibility through Design

There is considerable logic in attempting to break out of established urban patterns. For one thing, there is clearly a need for more urban space as the population continues to increase—accommodating urban man in the amount of space allotted to him in the past is no longer possible. Second, the agricultural revolution that has swelled the migration to cities also promises to make land suitable for urban development increasingly plentiful. Third, the technology for overcoming time and distance through a combination of rapid transport and instantaneous communications is now available, so that the means are at hand to release the urban population from age-old space constraints without the isolation and economic penalties that would have been incurred at an earlier time.

All over the globe people are moving out, in both haphazard and consciously planned efforts, to take advantage of the new opportunity to be urbanized without being imprisoned. The most impressive examples of a planned escape are to be found in the combination of urban renewal and new city building that is taking place everywhere. They provide encouraging signs that the slums can be rebuilt more quickly than had been thought, that new cities can be constructed to take care of the decongestion process, that modern transportation can help to make these efforts feasible, and that in the process of improving housing and the environment it may be possible to solve transportation problems at the same time.

New urban designs are revealing that the task of increasing urban mobility may not call for more transportation at all, but may depend more on such nontransportation solutions as the locations, densities, and aesthetics of everything being done to accommodate urban man. In other words, transportation demand derives from the design of the community itself and from its various life support systems. These include the places people live and work, the nature of the neighborhood and its surroundings, the power, water, and sanitation systems, and methods of supplying food, medical services, schools, and recreation. How these subsystems are located and interrelated determines what resources must be spent for transportation and whether this allocation of resources will make its maximum contribution to the community.

The relation between cities and transportation can be better understood by observing the design and operation of buildings. In a single building, approximately 10 percent of the enclosed space is devoted to transportation. Freight and passengers move with minimum congestion because both the structure and its transportation were integrally designed to perform that way. But any departure from the planned population and functions of a building will cause trouble. When the top floors of a building in New York were converted from low-density manufacturing and storage to high-density office space, the elevator system broke down in rush hours. Large numbers of people that were not planned for in the original design created a density of use higher than the transport system could cope with. The rush of arrivals at nine o'clock could be handled only by diverting this human overload to the freight elevators, where there was enough redundancy to overcome crowding on the passenger system.

Cities are in many respects like buildings that are poorly designed, are allowed to become unbalanced, or are generally without redundant transport capacity. Cities should be organized and planned as nearly as possible to achieve the goals and carry out the functions projected for their people. Transport systems should be designed to meet the expected generation of demand, and since it is in the nature of successful urban settlements to be dynamic, cities will change and departures from the original plan will have to be allowed for. At present the changes that take place in cities are usually not accompanied by any conscious effort to adjust transportation capabilities. Instead, the effects of greater densities or changes in zoning are absorbed in the social cost of congestion. That is, traffic is simply allowed to get worse, motorists are inconvenienced, transit riders suffer, and everyone experiences the effects either of an oversupply of apartments, office buildings, and other traffic generators or of poor selection of sites and consequent inconvenient interrelations.

Traffic problems and the ways of creating or avoiding them can be illustrated by spatial arrangements in a hospital, an analogy pointed out by the British Ministry of Transport. Hospitals are composed of wards, operating rooms, kitchens, and laboratories, and related activities are grouped together to reduce unnecessary movement and avoid through traffic where it has no reason to be. But if the building were badly designed so that food had to be wheeled through the operating room, it would be impossible to carry out the goals for which the structure was planned.[6] Similarly, a house built with the kitchen at one end and the dining room at the other is bound to create excessive traffic and loss of efficiency.

It is no different with cities. They too should be designed to provide convenient relations among related functions and to insulate what needs to be insulated. The purpose is to maximize efficiency; to minimize poor service, inconvenience, wasteful movement, and intrusions on peace and quiet.

There are now a growing number of buildings and building complexes throughout the world that have worked out freight and passenger transportation systems to suit the environment and to perform on a large scale with a high degree of effectiveness. Airports are good examples of development clusters with their own internal transport as well as connections with the outside. Some have advanced systems of internal circulation: moving belts for baggage, moving walkways for passengers (Geneva, Amsterdam), and a variety of service facilities that include hotels, restaurants, meeting rooms, theaters, and art exhibits (Orly in Paris). Some have connections to the center by rail (Brussels, Cleveland, and Tokyo).

Houston Intercontinental shows how a single airport can provide for its own cellular growth by simply duplicating a cluster of activity that is considered optimal in size. It was decided that maximum walking distance from automobile to airplane should be no greater than 600 feet. This criterion limited the capacity of the terminal to twenty jets at any one time. Beyond this level of activity, it was decided, there would have to be another terminal, and there are now two. In this way growth is assimilated by duplicating the basic unit rather than permitting increased activity to interfere with what is already completed and functioning well. A link between terminals is provided by minisubway with

6. *Traffic in Towns: A Study of the Long Term Problems of Traffic in Urban Areas,* Reports of the Steering Group and Working Group appointed by the Minister of Transport (London: Her Majesty's Stationery Office, 1963), p. 41.

seven-passenger cars moved by electric battery-powered tractors and automatically guided by magnetic equipment in the tunnel floor. The run of one-third of a mile, with a stop at the parking lot, takes four minutes. Four trains operating with two-minute headway can carry 650 seated persons an hour. It is also possible to walk through the tunnel. The total system suggests the physical layout of a regional city comprising pedestrian clusters connected by major transport routes.

The clustering of urban activity is most commonly found in large shopping centers and downtown redevelopment projects. Ala Moana Center in Honolulu covers fifty acres, three-fourths of it devoted to pedestrian malls, gardens, pools, landscaping, and parking. There are 155 stores employing 4,700 persons and a twenty-five-story building containing offices, medical centers, and other services. Newer shopping centers are entirely enclosed so that heated and air-conditioned walkways supply comfort and protection as well as attractive displays for pedestrians. In Europe the addition of housing to downtown shopping centers such as those in Rotterdam and Coventry suggests that this would be an important means of achieving some degree of self-containment for suburban shopping centers in the United States, adding to their interest and attraction and subtracting from the dependence on automobiles for shopping.

Clusters for living, working, and recreation have also been created in major slum clearance and redevelopment projects in many cities. Montreal's Westmont Square, two miles west of downtown, is a two-block pedestrian island assembled from forty-five parcels of land and converted into one harmonious development with all local transportation by foot or by elevator and escalator. There are two high-rise buildings for apartments, a third for office space. The lower concourse beneath the buildings contains fifty stores, underground parking, a theater, and a block-long pedestrian tunnel to the subway system connecting with the rest of the city.[7]

The renewed center of Stockholm is a much larger area that represents the same combined approach to transportation and buildings, with internal circulation by pedestrian walkway. Transit, rail lines, and parking are all underground, below the pedestrian mall. The pedestrian area contains stores, theaters, and restaurants, and nearby are five eighteen-

7. Ellen P. Berkeley, "Westmont Square," *Architectural Forum*, Vol. 131 (September 1969), pp. 85–86.

story office buildings. The connecting subway carries passengers between the center and the outlying new towns.

Many cities in the United States are extending the concept of the cluster in downtown redevelopment areas to obtain a mixture of activities that includes transportation and commercial, cultural, and living accommodations. The rebuilding of downtown St. Louis includes a boulevard and park, adjacent housing along pedestrian walkways, retail stores, offices, and the recreational facilities of the waterfront. Boston's Prudential Center, with railway, subway, parking, and expressway concealed beneath the pedestrian platform, provides a shopping center, hotel and convention site, and high-rise office complex. The addition of surrounding apartments has made it possible to live and work in a single area.

Another example of the partially self-contained and readily accessible cluster is New York's plan for Battery Park City on the Hudson River in Manhattan. This new city within the central city—the largest single real estate development in the country—will be built on a landfill of 100 acres to provide 21,000 apartments, 5 million square feet of office space, a hotel, a shopping area, parks, and recreation. A platform over the West Side Highway will convert a section of this elevated structure to a covered roadway. Streets and transit will be underground and out of sight, and tens of thousands of people will conduct most of their daily trips within the area itself, by elevator, corridor, and walkway.

In London, much larger housing estates, some for as many as 100,000 people, combine transport with extensive community facilities to produce traffic-free clusters in the middle of the city. The Pepys estate on the Thames, occupying the site of a former naval installation, is a community of high-rise and garden apartments integrated by a pedestrian circulation system, with schools and playgrounds, shopping areas, health centers, and underground freight delivery. The Greater London Council has provided dwellings for one million Londoners in these "new town" neighborhoods within the old city.

Thus multipurpose urban clusters fulfilling a variety of functions can help to maximize access and minimize time wasted on transportation. Proximity may be the best substitute for mobility. Freedom of access can often best be supplied by transportation on foot, with both horizontal and vertical aids to walking. The important result is to substitute large buildings or groups of buildings for separate and unrelated structures that treat problems of access and circulation as external factors. These complexes solve many of their transport problems internally by grouping complementary economic activities, by combining public and private investments in area-wide projects, by joint land acquisition, and by combining programs of housing, recreation, transport, and commercial development.

In existing cities it may be possible to compensate in part for present unplanned locations of economic activities by extending the idea of the cluster to help organize urban transport collections and deliveries. One such method has been proposed for the New York metropolitan region, where 430,000 trucks perform local trucking services and generate 11 percent of all vehicle-miles driven in the area. One-third of these trucks do not move at all on any given weekday, and of those moving, about half carry no load. The total cost of truck deliveries is about $2 billion a year.[8] The proposed solution is to divide the region into centers of truck activity averaging about three square miles each, where off-street sorting terminals would combine small shipments for delivery to other terminals. By consolidating shipments into twelve-ton loads, it is believed that transport between clusters could be reduced 90 percent. Substantial savings could be achieved in each of the local terminal areas as well, where the present pick-up and delivery system is so disorganized that it generates 22.6 miles of travel a ton, even though the average length of haul from origin to destination is only 5 miles a ton.

## European Planned Communities

A point of considerable sophistication has been reached in the planned communities of Europe through the large-scale application of urban design to achieve ease of access and the effective use of transport investments as an integral part of urban structure. These communities illustrate how transport facilities can supply the sites for new housing, insulate living space from through traffic, meet the needs of pedestrians, and provide nearby jobs and recreation. The underlying idea is the same as in buildings or complexes of buildings: to balance transport capacity with anticipated transport demands, to solve transport requirements by making things accessible, and to make transport investments add to the quality of the urban area.

8. See Tri-State Transportation Commission, "Truck Freight in the Tri-State Region" (TSTC, 1969; processed), Vol. 1, p. 2; Vol. 2, p. 14.

All planned communities of recent vintage are motorized cities, but their design and operation also show concern for people who are not car owners. The new towns in Britain have been able both to achieve spaciousness through the availability of the automobile and to attract people who feel isolated without a car. For those not owning or driving cars, good bus service is offered along with the option of walking short distances on pedestrian pathways.

All the new towns demonstrate with varying degrees of success that it is possible to measure within reasonable margins the traffic-generating and traffic-attracting characteristics of various uses of land. In each case it has been assumed that much of the repetitive daily travel of the family can be accommodated without the investment of large sums of money for high-speed transport, simply by rearrangements that shorten distances. The nearby grocery, newsstand, school, church, community house, playground, and park are trade-offs that substitute accessibility for mobility. Those shopping in the town center can choose between public transport and private car, but in neither case is the motor vehicle allowed to intrude. The home-to-work problem has been the major obstacle to a congestion-free community, but the location of employment opportunities away from congested centers and the option of living within short distances of work have pointed the way toward solution.

Britain's Stevenage is a planned community thirty miles north of London. It was begun before the full impact of the automobile revolution was realized, but the automobile has been a major factor in the community's growth and has dictated the changes necessary in a motorized society. Six large neighborhoods of 10,000 persons each were built in a semicircle around the town center, and each of them is provided with its own shopping center of fifteen to thirty shops and two subsidiary centers of four to twelve shops. The main shopping area of Stevenage is reached by automobile, bus, or pedestrian walkway. By 1967, 18,000 industrial workers were employed in the 400 acres devoted to industry on the west side of the town. More than 85 percent of all employed residents worked inside the town.

Patterns of automobile and transit use are quite different from what is experienced in conventional unplanned cities. Of all trips made within the town limits, 43 percent are on foot, 24 percent by automobile, and 20 percent by bicycle or other two-wheeled vehicle. Only 13 percent are by bus. Where distances are short, both old and young can make their way on foot. On a typical Saturday, nearly half of all shopping trips are made in the neighborhood. The rest are destined for the larger town center, to which half of the customers walk. Three-quarters of all school-children walk to school and one-eighth ride bicycles on bicycle pathways free of automobiles.

The design of Stevenage has cut down considerably on the per capita mileage traveled. Three out of four trips cover less than two miles. In the outer ring of conventional large cities in England, only one out of four daily trips is that short, and a third of all city journeys are longer than five miles one way. Little more than a tenth of the trips made by Stevenage residents are that long, and most of those who work in the town live within a mile or two of their jobs.[9]

Another alternative to congested living is Scotland's East Kilbride, nine miles and thirty-five minutes by commuter railway from Glasgow. Total area of the town is 10,000 acres, of which only 2,500 are being developed and the rest left in farmland. The projected population is 70,000 with possible further expansion to 100,000. Industrial estates in East Kilbride employ 20,000 workers from within the community, producing such items as jet engines, telephone equipment, electric razors, record players, and thermostats.

The town center of 44 acres has been designed for pedestrians only, and the main highways go around it. Loading and unloading are underground. Pedestrians are provided with bridges and underpasses across major thoroughfares, and in the center itself they are protected from the rain by large overhanging roofs. The shopping area includes a moving picture theater, hotels, office buildings, and an adjacent park with playing fields, swimming pool, and youth center. The next section of the town center will be fully enclosed and air-conditioned.

In the surrounding area there are neighborhood shops mainly for customers on foot which provide the daily necessities from the baker, butcher, and grocery store. Some neighborhood shopping areas include a health center, churches, and restaurants. Each neighborhood also contains a primary school and ten acres of playing fields and open space for every thousand residents.

Street plans make a major contribution to the favorable impression created by East Kilbride. Landscaping and the use of remnants of land along the right-of-way for small parks add considerably to utility and

9. Raymond C. Bunker, "Travel and Land Use in Stevenage" (University of Birmingham, Department of Transportation and Environmental Planning, 1966; processed).

appearance. The underground installation of telephone and electric wires along with the planting of 320,000 shade trees make the transportation network more attractive. The street layout avoids uniformity, making use of dead ends by traversing them with pedestrian walkways or stairways. Apartments often span the walkways. The pedestrian streets introduce belts of green throughout the city, and regular maintenance crews keep grounds and housing in good condition.

The automobile was specifically taken into account in Scotland's later new town of Cumbernauld, one of the so-called Mark II towns, which attempt to prevent traffic from disrupting the life of the city. Cumbernauld has abandoned the division of the city into neighborhoods and has instead built its housing around the town center at sufficiently high densities to enable more people to get to the main center on foot. The compact nature of the city is achieved by an average density of 85 persons an acre, and by the construction of high-cost expressways. These primary roads cost about twice as much a mile as was paid for the major arterials in other new towns. However, their shorter mileage plus the large population served has resulted in per capita costs for vehicular roadways (exclusive of cul-de-sac streets serving residents) only slightly below the average highway costs for all new towns.[10]

A unique feature of Cumbernauld is the half-mile-long eight-story town center, where all shopping and related activities can be carried out in a one-stop commercial and recreational area. At the top of this complex building are penthouse apartments, a restaurant, central library, meeting halls, and recreation facilities. On the lower levels are a department store, health center, eating places, hotel, offices, day nursery, banks, and more recreation facilities. Beneath the structure are roadways, bus terminals, and parking areas.

In all of these efforts it is the combination of transport and buildings that produces the structure of the community and contributes to its character. The effect is to create roominess in the same amount of space that for unplanned urban areas of the same size would be likely to cause serious deficiencies in open space and aesthetics, as well as undesirable crowding and unnecessary traffic. The new towns have made transport facilities play multiple roles effectively, and have applied land-use planning to lessening transport problems.

10. Frederic J. Osborn and Arnold Whittick, *The New Towns: Answer to Megalopolis* (McGraw-Hill, 1964), pp. 376–89.

It is now recognized that cities must be considerably larger than the early British experiments if they are to afford the necessary diversity of economic activity and be interesting communities. The newest new towns will be twice the size of their predecessors. A wide range of living conditions will be provided to attract a variety of residents, and attention will be focused on education, health, and recreation. Social planning is emphasized to overcome the stress on physical planning, which is concerned more with geometry than with people, "as if the major purpose of a city was to present a symmetrical and pleasing spectacle when seen from an airplane."[11] While design is important, Herbert Gans reminds us that people have other problems, including money, health, husband-wife relationships, and parent-children problems, which have to be resolved by such methods as the redistribution of income, opportunities for women to use their time advantageously, the creation of day-care centers, and places for adolescents to spend their leisure hours physically removed from their parents. "This kind of planning would require the planner either to become a sociologist and psychologist or to work closely with behavioural scientists to observe what problems people are trying to solve and what goals they are seeking."[12]

The evolution of Britain's new-town thinking furnishes valuable lessons for introducing social factors into urban design. The Mark I towns, such as Harlow, were conceived as relatively small, physically well defined, and self-contained. But self-containment disappeared with the automobile, and the Mark II towns, built to reflect the trend toward universal car ownership, made the idea of self-containment even less practical. Later, therefore, the Mark III series of new communities recognized that the automobile age had introduced a new freedom to live, work, and shop wherever desired, and that this made it impossible to confine new town residents to their own community or to protect against automobile invasion from the outside.

The need for a much larger population in new communities plus almost universal car ownership threatened greater congestion for the Mark III towns, such as Redditch and Milton Keynes, which needed to be well supplied with public transportation as well as designed for those who would use cars for decentralized employment and shopping. In Redditch, for example, no one has to walk more than a third of a mile

11. Herbert J. Gans, "Planning for People, Not Buildings," *Environment and Planning*, Vol. 1, No. 1 (1969), p. 33.
12. Ibid., p. 40.

to public transport, but parking is also available for 1.4 cars per family. Rapid change also made it clear that new communities would have to be very flexible in design, ready to respond to an assortment of unpredictable pressures. They could not be designed with the idea of permanency or resistance to change.

The Mark III towns have introduced social considerations into housing types and public services. They have attempted to overcome the "new town blues" by furnishing a wider variety of housing and job opportunities, by mixing land uses, and by resisting single-class neighborhoods. Plans include community-wide health services and recreation, and methods of reducing the gap between high- and low-income families through education, the acquisition of skills, and information systems that promote economic and social contacts.

To illustrate, the 21,000-acre tract that will be the new Milton Keynes has been designed to accommodate 250,000 residents. The estimated total outlay over a twenty-five-year period for land acquisition and construction (as of 1970) was $1.7 billion, of which 48 percent will be obtained from the Milton Keynes Development Corporation, 24 percent from local authorities, and 28 percent from the private sector. Transportation and communications account for 5 percent of capital expenditures and 11 percent of the total available land area. This amounts to ten transport acres for each thousand people.[13]

The plan for Milton Keynes calls for seven conditions to be met:

>Easy access to all the parts and activities of the city
>Freedom of choice between automobile and public transport
>A high quality of public transport
>Use of the automobile without congestion
>Flexibility in the transport system to allow for change
>Transport that is safe and nonpolluting
>Freedom for the pedestrian

It is assumed that by the end of the century 90 percent of all residents will own a car, and that total passenger movements will be divided between automobile and public carriers in the ratio of 80–20. The city is expected to house 120,000 workers.

13. *The Plan for Milton Keynes*, Vol. 1: Presented by the Milton Keynes Development Corporation to the Minister of Housing and Local Government (London: MKDC, 1970), p. 71 and Table 1; Vol. 2: Report of Evidence Presented by the Consultants to the Milton Keynes Development Corporation (MKDC, 1970), p. 274.

Five general urban forms were considered, and transportation requirements were estimated for each one. They included (1) concentrated central employment, (2) employment concentrated around the periphery, (3) a division of employment between center and periphery, (4) two major employment centers at opposite locations on the periphery, and (5) a dispersed pattern of job locations. The mileage of necessary transport routes and the volume of travel required for each plan are shown in Table 3-1.

TABLE 3-1. *Transport Requirements for Alternative Urban Plans, Milton Keynes, England, 1970*

| Urban plan | Daily passenger-miles of commuter travel (thousands) | Total street lanes required (miles) |
|---|---|---|
| Concentrated central employment | 268 | 340 |
| Perimeter employment | 319 | 240 |
| Combination of 1 and 2 | 290 | 220 |
| Two peripheral centers of employment | 340 | 385 |
| Dispersed employment | 272 | 170 |

Source: *The Plan for Milton Keynes*, Vol. 2: Report of Evidence Presented by the Consultants to the Milton Keynes Development Corporation (London: MKDC, 1970), pp. 281–82.

It was concluded that there was no marked transport disadvantage in either plan 3 or plan 5, and a combination of the two was adopted in the final design.

Highly significant for the motorized city is the open-ended nature of the newest new towns, which recognize the need for expansion, the possibilities that population growth will alter land uses, and the certainty that levels of income and patterns of living and of leisure-time activities will change. Thus it is no longer possible to think of fixed boundaries or static community plans. The Mark III towns attempt to furnish guides to growth rather than impose conditions that would dictate an inflexible growth process.[14]

Sweden provides an example of metropolitan development that encompasses both the old city and the suburbs. In Stockholm a combined attack has been launched on congestion by a combination of central city renewal and the creation of urban satellites about ten miles out to contain the displaced population and provide for growth. It has been

14. See Richard Llewelyn-Davies, "Town Design," in *The Town Planning Review*, Vol. 37 (October 1966), pp. 157–72.

*Farsta's pedestrian shopping center*
Bror Karlsson/Swedish Information Service

*Stockholm's Vallingby, a planned urban satellite*
Swedish Information Service

public policy since the turn of the century for the city to buy property outside its borders in anticipation of long-term growth, with the purpose of guiding the exodus. Many suburban areas, not immediately used for urban development, were purchased and leased back to the owners to be continued in agricultural uses until needed, and the earnings used to pay interest on the funds borrowed for acquisition.

These publicly owned lands have subsequently been the means of protecting rural areas around Stockholm from undesirable development and have provided nearby sites for satellite communities. As early as 1941 plans were made for constructing a rapid transit system in the public land belt between the old and the new communities, so located as to provide the essential public transport links to the future satellite suburbs authorized in the Stockholm master plan. Suburban centers were built around each station as the fingers of the transit system extended outward, with main centers established at some of these stations to serve the needs of several smaller communities. The result is a series of small suburbs of 10,000 to 15,000 people, and an occasional main center of 50,000 to 100,000 people, all with easy access to Stockholm. In the past two decades, eighteen suburban units have been built, clustered into three groups around main centers. There are about 250,000 people living in these planned suburbs.

The Stockholm satellites were initiated before the preeminence of the automobile, when it was assumed that the relation of satellite to central city would be maintained primarily by rail. Since then Sweden has become the number one automotive nation of Europe, and this has brought about substantial changes in design and in the possibilities for larger settlements than previously envisioned. Prosperity has also introduced doubts about the wisdom of emphasizing multiple family dwellings with limited space. But Stockholm and its satellites demonstrate a logical solution to congestion in which urban renewal, new suburbs, and good public transport are all essential ingredients in building the regional city. The transport system is tailored to meet a calculated demand, and the land uses and activities generating the demand are influenced both by the developments of housing and economic activity and by the brakes on urban growth applied through the preservation of public open spaces.

There are other European examples of comprehensive community planning and large-scale city building. In Belgrade, for example, the response to central city congestion was to move across the Danube and erect a whole new city on 10,000 acres of agricultural land. High-rise apartments of modern design and colorful exteriors house 100,000 persons, and 40 percent of the area is in parklands, with broad green spaces along the riverfront for museums, exhibition halls, and public buildings. The old city, however, is still the major focus of employment, with only one out of five new city residents also working in the new location. The result has been to intensify commuter traffic across the Danube even though emphasis is on the use of public transport, including the commuter railway.

Another planned community immediately adjacent to an established city is Esposizione Universale Roma (E.U.R.), which is only fifteen to twenty minutes by rapid transit from the center of Rome and close to the airport and the Mediterranean. This city of 100,000 has attractive high-rise offices and apartments, government ministries, exhibition halls, hotels, restaurants, shops, and housing. At the center an artificial lake is surrounded by promenades and gardens, and the subway station opens onto the lakefront. Large parking areas, which have been successfully camouflaged by landscaping, are provided at the city's two metro stops. Because this satellite was started more than thirty years ago, it has a seasoned look not yet achieved by most planned cities.

France has designated eight growth centers in a nationwide regional urbanization plan to counter the attractions of Paris. At the same time the construction of three major new communities has been started in the Paris area itself, with two others to be built; and ten new communities are planned or have been started in less congested parts of the country. The growth centers, or poles of development, given investment priority include Lyon, Grenoble, Marseille, Lille, Toulouse, and Strasbourg. The objective is to decentralize in urban centers with a population of a million or more. Planned urban dispersal is being encouraged by subsidies to industry for equipment purchases, loans on favorable terms, reduced taxes, and government investments in related infrastructure. There are also restrictions on new industrial development in the Paris region.[15]

### Asia's Experiments in Urban Design

More spectacular evidence of the coming shift from conventional urbanization to the planned community is provided by the accomplish-

15. See *France Actuelle*, Vol. 18 (Oct. 1, 1969).

ments of new cities in Asia. An impressive attempt to apply new city principles to the building and rebuilding of large urban areas is found in Singapore's slum clearance and redevelopment, combined with its planned satellite cities. This combination is solving transportation as well as living problems through the creation of a modern center city and peripheral new communities of 200,000 population and more, in which the proximity of workers' flats to stores, schools, and industrial employment is eliminating much of the overcrowding of the old community.

Singapore's development plan consists of a network of housing estates, or satellite towns—a series of dispersed concentrations to replace the planless arrangement of the old city. In the short space of one decade, low-cost housing in high-rise flats has been provided for 600,000 residents, or 30 percent of the population. Most of the new housing is in eight major housing estates located five to six miles from the center, containing community facilities and local industries. More satellites will be added as the conversion of British military bases provides additional new town sites with much of the needed infrastructure already in place. Each community is planned to be partially self-contained by having industrial and commercial employment within easy reach of good housing. The simultaneous clearing and restoration of downtown Singapore is possible because new quarters are ready for displaced residents in the satellite towns. The Raffles International Center, the next major downtown renewal project, combines several city blocks to create a center of luxury apartments, shops, conference halls, recreation facilities, and offices. Transportation in such a complex is by walkway, open court, and elevator. A similar complex for education and training will be established on a new location to which the university will eventually be moved.

The approach to solving transportation problems and at the same time housing, community development, and economic growth problems is demonstrated by the new satellite city of Jurong, in the southwest corner of Singapore. The town site was prepared by bulldozing the surrounding hills into the coastal swampland, which will ultimately make available 12,000 acres close to the waterfront. Construction of the city began in 1961. By 1971 there were 284 factories in production, with about 35,000 jobs. The target is 500 factories and 70,000 jobs. Approximately 12,000 housing units have been constructed and about a quarter of those who work in Jurong live there. The objective is to have 60 to 70 percent of the work force in residence. The others are expected to commute by bus and car.

*High-rise living for low-income families in Singapore's Queenstown*
Embassy of Singapore

*Play space in Singapore*
*Embassy of Singapore*

Jurong was created by act of Parliament, under the jurisdiction of the Ministry of Finance. The ministry makes loans for housing with repayment over sixty years and provides thirty-year construction loans to factories at 6 percent interest. Large tax yields from new industries more than compensate for the subsidy. By 1980 Jurong may have 400,000 residents, and extensive facilities to attract and hold families in the new city are already built, including a 700-acre park, artificial lake, golf course, bird sanctuary, modern shopping centers, and a variety of cultural facilities.

The physical planning of Singapore, therefore, is based on two complementary ideas. One is the dispersal of urban concentrations to avoid a single high-density urban center producing unmanageable problems of housing, lack of amenities, and intolerable traffic congestion. The other is the arrangement of land use within the separate clusters in such ways as will reduce the volume of daily travel requirements, especially commuting to work, and thus solve transport problems through urban design.

The Singapore development plan has the underlying objectives of providing access to lower-cost land to reduce the pressures on already developed land and to carry out the national commitment to furnish adequate housing and community facilities that meet the needs of all residents. From a transportation point of view, the Singapore model of an urbanized region reflects much of British and Swedish new town and urban redevelopment experience. As in British new towns, the Singapore housing estates attempt to reduce average travel requirements by making it possible to walk to school, shopping, and recreation, and by providing employment close to residential areas.

Many trips are taken between satellites and central city, however, for unlike the British new towns, which are farther removed from previously established cities and which were originally (and mistakenly) designed to be virtually self-supporting, Singapore's new towns are meant to be part of a regional system of settlements. Their inhabitants may or may not choose to work close to home. Since the new settlements are close to the old city, their role is more like that of Stockholm's satellites, which are within ten miles of the city center and partially dependent on it.

The merit of Singapore's regional plan is that open space or low-density development is maintained between clusters, so there are relatively clear channels of communication connecting a network of urban developments that achieve dispersal without sprawl and concentration without congestion. Within the concentrations, urban design and building arrangements solve much of the local transportation problem, leaving the major transport requirements to be met by the connections from one town to the next and from satellite to central city.

The Singapore program is carried out by a Housing and Development Board created for the purpose, and has been made possible by a series of government loans repayable with interest, and by allocations of government funds that are made available to all public corporations for urban services. Building on a large scale kept unit costs down, and building quickly made possible an early start in repaying government loans through rentals. More recently, the board has been selling apartments under a home ownership scheme that provides long-term loans. Additional revenue is obtained from leases to industrial establishments and from the sale of land to private developers in downtown Singapore, where the slum clearance and renewal program has allowed the assembling of large parcels. These the Development Board sells to the highest bidder for the construction of specific projects such as hotels, office buildings, department stores, and garages.

Income of the Housing and Development Board from rents and sales in 1970 was sufficient to pay administration and maintenance costs of the new communities, property taxes, and $10 million in interest and repayment of government loans. Cumulative deficits amounted to $12 million, which represents the subsidy for low-cost housing: 33 cents a month for each resident of the new cities and housing estates.[16]

In the current five-year plan, 1971–75, Singapore is stepping up its housing program to duplicate the feat of the first ten years in half the time. Although it might be assumed that to accommodate the entire population of a city in quality housing and environment would entail too great an economic burden, the Singapore experience suggests a different conclusion. While the program has transformed the city and provided immeasurably better living conditions for low-income families, there has been a simultaneous improvement in all aspects of the economy. Between 1960 and 1970, Singapore more than doubled its per capita gross domestic product, government revenues tripled, and consumers now spend twice as much on housing as they did in 1960, but

16. Data from Housing and Development Board, Singapore, *Annual Report* 1970, pp. 40–41. See also *First Decade in Public Housing*, 1960–69 (HDB, 1970).

also more than twice as much on transportation, mostly for cars.[17] Altogether the output of the manufacturing sector is three times the 1960 level, and there are 200,000 more jobs than there were twelve years ago.

There are other examples of planned cities in Asia where growth has been achieved without increasing congestion and with substantial gains toward a quality environment. One is the new city of Makati, a spacious planned community adjacent to Manila, with a population of 200,000. Makati has broad boulevards, shopping centers, off-street parking, and control over land-use arrangements and densities that help to create an attractive and efficient city with minimum congestion. A private company owned the land, developed the master plan, and financed the project, including water supply, sewage treatment plant, and street system. In the central commercial area all purchasers of property had to agree to build in three years, to use reinforced concrete, to construct at least six stories, to light the building exteriors at night, and to provide air-conditioning. Oil- and gas-burning furnaces are banned. Forty percent of commercial lots have to be reserved for parking in the rear, and ultimately for multifloor parking structures. Up to 70 percent of residential property is left vacant for lawns and gardens.

Makati was once a blighted town of shanties, and the new city project involved both new development and redevelopment. In twenty-five years population has quadrupled. More than 2,000 firms have located offices or manufacturing plants there, and in ten years municipal income increased more than 100-fold. The plan has reconciled urbanization and motorization in a community relatively free of congestion and with a high-quality environment.[18]

Asia's planned communities can hardly be said to have met with unqualified success. Makati, for example, did little or nothing to house low-income families, and in Singapore the density and height of structures do not always suit the tastes of the occupants. A good balance between housing and employment has really not been achieved anywhere. In Singapore, for example, where the Housing and Development Board was responsible for Queenstown and other satellites, concern was principally with a rapid improvement in housing, and too few work places were included in the new community. Recently an effort has been made to correct this by the establishment of factories for rent

17. Department of Statistics, Singapore, *Yearbook of Statistics, Singapore,* 1970.
18. See Stephen Espie, "The Miracle of Makati," in U.S. Information Service (Manila), *Free World,* Vol. 17 (June 1968), pp. 20–35.

to small industries. The reverse was true of Jurong, which was built by the Economic Development Board and, since 1968, the Jurong Town Corporation, both agencies concerned with industrial development. The result was extensive factory construction and less concern for housing and related facilities. Workers have been reluctant to move out to Jurong, partly because of the distance from the developed center of Singapore, but also because of the pollution from plywood and petrochemical factories, the lack of amenities early in the construction period, and the feeling that there is neither community nor variety in this spread-out industrial complex. As a consequence only about 25 percent of the work force lives and works in Jurong. But the present situation can be expected to correct itself as the time and cost of travel to and from Singapore discourage commutation, and if pollution abatement and the completion of various urban amenities make the new town more attractive.

In Malaysia the satellite city of Petaling Jaya, which accommodates some 70,000 people outside Kuala Lumpur, is evidence of the importance of achieving a good balance between housing and employment. Heavy commuter congestion has resulted as workers living in Kuala Lumpur stream into the industrial estates of Petaling Jaya in the morning and residents of Petaling Jaya drive into the commercial center of the capital city to their employment in offices. The reason for this heavy cross-hauling is that Petaling Jaya was not originally conceived as a complete community. During World War II it was a refugee camp, and this earlier section of the city now consists of modest housing for low-income groups, for whom there is employment in nearby industrial estates. Most housing in Petaling Jaya, however, is not for factory workers but for middle-income families who moved to Petaling Jaya because the new community offered a chance to buy land at a reasonable price and build on it. But there was no office building to provide employment for these householders, and they continued to commute to government and commercial offices in Kuala Lumpur. The resulting lessons may prove useful in designing the new state capital to be built nearby, which must minimize the volume of commuting if the highways in the area are to cope with the heavy automotive traffic.

Significant beginnings have thus been made toward the development of new cities in Asia, with varying degrees of success. The classic early example is New Delhi, with its contrast between a modern government center and the nearby slums of the ancient city. In Pakistan, a planned retreat from the congestion of Karachi, 950 miles to the south, is the new capital of Islamabad, where government employees live and work in an environment far superior to that of the old city. India can point to Le Corbusier's Chandigarh, the capital of the Punjab, as powerful testimony that man can be saved from the squalor of the accidental city. The contrast between Chandigarh and nearby Ludhiana is as startling as the view of Scotland's East Kilbride after Glasgow. With all their shortcomings, the planned cities are demonstrating what can be done in the future to improve conditions for Asia's rapidly expanding urban population.

## Planned Cities for the United States

Although official counts tell us that more than forty new communities were completed or substantially begun in the United States during the sixties, the statistics are misleading. The American version of the new town is primarily a suburban housing and recreation development rather than a whole community. The new American cities have all been undertaken by private developers, with limited government aid, limited economic base, and little concern for the low-income family. The typical suburban complexes in the United States are not aimed at rectifying the poor housing and other disadvantages of low-income groups or at alleviating congestion by matching residential and industrial development. They were built to serve the market for middle- and upper-income housing, and as private efforts they have been able to benefit only marginally from public support. Their size and location have been dependent on where it was possible to assemble the land, and their relation to the region has been only incidentally considered.[19]

There are, however, two major new cities now being built in the United States: Reston, Virginia, and Columbia, Maryland. Columbia, which is being built on 14,000 acres, a site about the size of Manhattan, will accommodate 110,000 people when completed in 1981.[20] It is believed to be large enough to support needed urban institutions, and it is divided into forty pedestrian-oriented neighborhoods. Like Milton

19. See AIP Task Force on New Communities, *New Communities: Challenge for Today*, Background Paper No. 2 (Washington: American Institute of Planners, 1968).
20. See American City Corporation, *City Building: Experience, Trends and New Directions* (Columbia, Md.: ACC, 1971).

Keynes, Columbia is making a conscious effort to meet social requirements by developing a network of nonprofit institutions such as public
schools, health centers, libraries, and religious structures. While these
institutions do not make money, they bring quality and diversity to life
in Columbia, and the effort is paying off by attracting specialized
schools, colleges, and institutional innovations in public education and
health care.

Land acquisition for Columbia involved 140 separate transactions, an
average purchase price of $1,500 an acre, and a total land price of some
$23 million. Financing was achieved through a joint venture of the
developer and a life insurance company, with later support from a bank
and other insurance companies. After the site had been acquired, preliminary plans were approved at a public hearing and zoning was obtained from the county government through a new town district ordinance. The Planning Board of the county approved the final plans,
and the formal opening was in 1967. By 1971 there were about 12,000
residents, 36 industrial plants, some 100 business establishments, and
more than 5,000 jobs.

Reston, which is eighteen miles from Washington, D.C., had about
the same population as Columbia as of early 1971, and is scheduled for
a population of 78,000 when completed. Land for Reston was obtained
primarily from the purchase of one tract of 6,750 acres, with some later
additional purchases. Average cost an acre was $2,000. The Gulf Oil
Company and insurance interests have been the principal sources of
financial support.

A new era of government-assisted new city development for the
United States was introduced by the New Communities Act of 1968,
which includes a federal guarantee to provide private developers with
the long-term low-interest financing necessary to carry them through the
early construction period. New communities eligible for this assistance
are not restricted as to either size or location. They can be new cities in
old cities, expansions of existing cities, satellites within metropolitan
areas, or new cities located without reference to any existing city. Developers, to be eligible for assistance, are required to submit a comprehensive development plan that includes a combination of residences and
work places, a variety of housing for all income groups, social services,
and all the elements needed for long-term economic growth and environmental quality.

In the Housing and Urban Development Act of 1970, these aids to new city building are extended to public agencies as well as private, and the federal government guarantees payment of bonds issued for land acquisition, schools, and hospitals.

The new city of Jonathan, Minnesota, was the first to benefit under the New Communities Act of 1968. This city, designed for a population of 50,000, is located on 8,000 acres twenty-four miles and thirty minutes from downtown Minneapolis by expressway. Each of five villages will house from 5,000 to 7,000 people, with high-density living provided in the town center built over the railway and highway systems. The town includes a 3,000-acre learning center containing many institutions for higher education. Jonathan will be developed over a twenty-year period with factory-built modular housing. A wide-spectrum coaxial system using cable television, computer, and other forms of information communication to provide community health and education services is planned.

In Minneapolis the new community Cedar Riverside will be a "new town in town" for 30,000 people within a 340-acre urban renewal project. Possibilities being studied are an experimental education program and comprehensive health services, and the pairing of the newer town with Jonathan for the purpose of exchanging facilities and expertise in the arts, education, health, and social services.

Another new city between Dallas and Fort Worth will contain 60,000 people, with housing for all income levels, complete health facilities, and a variety of employment opportunities. In Illinois, Park Forest South, thirty miles from Chicago, will be built for 110,000 people, with a substantial number of units for low- and moderate-income residents, twenty-six schools, a college, a multilevel linear town center, pedestrian transport systems, community health services, and an industrial park.

Welfare Island in New York City's East River, a new pedestrian-oriented city for 20,000, part of the New York State Urban Development Corporation's program, will introduce a number of innovations. One is electric minitransit that will enable the public school system to use the whole island as its educational campus. Day-care and primary school units will be interrelated with residences and provided with direct pedestrian access to surrounding open spaces and parks. As they become older, children will move beyond their home base to other learning, activity, and cultural centers throughout the island, using transit, bicycles on bicycle paths, or the walkway system.

Other new city developments are being undertaken in the United

States by partnerships of real estate firms and large corporations with systems development capabilities, including housing, education, health, transportation, and other city-building components. These efforts at new city building will be reinforced if state governments succeed in creating urban development corporations or similar institutions.

The transfer of new city technology from the United Kingdom to the United States is being furthered by the selection of a British city-planning firm to design the new city of Amherst for the New York State Urban Development Corporation. Amherst is a residential suburb of Buffalo which will be the site of a new community to serve the needs of the adjacent relocated New York State University campus. The purpose of the new community is to allow families dependent on the university to live as close as possible, at an acceptable cost, in an appropriate environment.

Without specifically planning for this expansion, the new campus would inevitably be surrounded by ugly housing developments and commercial sprawl, the university and its environment would be damaged beyond repair, and the needs for good housing and convenient community facilities would not be met.

The Urban Development Corporation's total program for New York State envisages that half of the 5 million people to be added to the state's urban population over the next thirty years will have the opportunity to live in new communities. The total land area saved by avoiding conventional sprawl would be 842,000 acres, about three times the combined area of the state's major cities: Buffalo, Rochester, Syracuse, Albany, Yonkers, and New York.[21] Assuming average land acquisition costs at $1,500 an acre, the savings realized by planned communities as contrasted with unplanned sprawl would total $1.25 billion in land alone.

According to New York State estimates, the cost of locating half a million people in planned communities would total $9.1 billion, of which $7.3 billion would be private costs, mostly for housing, industry, commercial facilities, and power. Public costs would be only $1.8 billion, of which one-third would be for land acquisition and land improvement and another third for education. Much of the outlay for planned communities would be incurred in any case for conventional

21. *New Communities for New York*, A Report Prepared by the New York State Urban Development Corporation and the New York State Office of Planning Coordination (1970), pp. 58–59.

growth patterns, but planned urbanization would offer large benefits through an assured pleasant and congestion-free environment with ample services and amenities.

### Planned versus Unplanned Communities

Most urban settlements planned as units are surprisingly like conventional cities in density and in the proportion of land devoted to various purposes. But the effect is very different because of the concept and plan. New cities around London were designed for an average density of about 11,000 persons a square mile of urbanized area.[22] This is roughly comparable to central city densities in Berkeley, California, Pittsburgh, Pennsylvania, and Providence, Rhode Island. However, much of the total designated new town area is not urbanized, but is left in open uses. When this total area is used as the basis of calculation, the density of British new towns is comparable to that of Miami, Florida.

Population densities for American cities in general are lower than those of British planned communities, yet the latter give the impression of far more open space and roominess, so much so that many critics charge them with being wasteful of land. They seem to be low-density settlements when in fact they are not. One might suppose that differences in the proportions of various land uses account for the lack of crowding and the favorable visual impression. But most of the differences are minimal. Cities in the United States, use somewhat less space for housing than do British planned communities (40 percent in the United States, 49 percent in Britain) and slightly less space for public recreation areas (18 percent as against 20 percent in Britain). There is more land per house lot in U.S. cities, however, and more land that is undeveloped and unused. Much of this is in vacant lots that add nothing to the community and often detract from it substantially.[23]

Unlike unplanned U.S. cities, therefore, the planned British cities make use of all the land in the urbanized area, and undeveloped land is

22. Calculated from data in Robin H. Best, *Land for New Towns: A Study of Land Use, Densities, and Agricultural Displacement* (London: Town and Country Planning Association, 1964), App. 2, p. 58.

23. A 1961 Bureau of the Census report showed that there were 6 million vacant lots inside American cities. *Hearings Before the National Commission on Urban Problems*, Vol. 4 (1968), pp. 226–28.

restricted to large tracts outside the development area, providing open space and an adjacent rural setting. The use of row houses makes more land available for recreation and parks, and the arrangement of housing makes fewer streets necessary. The average amount of space devoted to streets in U.S. cities ranges from 25 to 30 percent, whereas the so-called residual uses in British new towns (including streets but also railway and other properties) average only 13 percent.

Aside from the streets, the proportions of land use dedicated to various purposes do not differ greatly between planned and unplanned communities. In Boston, Massachusetts, for instance, housing absorbs 60 percent of the total developed land (again, the British new towns use 49 percent). About 8 percent of Boston's area is devoted to industrial and commercial uses; British new towns average 10 percent. The major difference is the location, physical arrangement, and interrelation of land uses, and the concern for the environment. In planned urban areas there is not the same concentration of employment at the center, and there is more close-in living. Industrial parks are on the periphery, close to good housing in pleasing neighborhoods. The conventional unplanned city may have more living and working space per capita, but because it is disorganized, transportation must compensate for resulting inadequacies—the long distances that have to be traveled because large areas of bad environment limit the places people are willing to live in. On the other hand, planned communities suffer less traffic congestion despite the relatively small percentage of area devoted to streets because convenient land-use relations provide easier access, trips are shorter, and there is considerable reliance on walking.

The same number of families can be housed in about half the space in planned communities by designing residential neighborhoods in clusters, surrounded by open land, instead of in conventional small lots that chop up the available space into plots that are not fully used. The difference between the two approaches is illustrated by comparing planned communities with conventional developments. The normal way of subdividing 112 acres of land is quite different from what is accomplished by clustering, as shown in Table 3-2.

Open space is gained in the cluster plan because groups of townhouses can have a common green and playground in the center, and the land between groupings can be used for recreation. The rest of the open space can be left as countryside with minimum landscaping. Unfortunately, says William H. Whyte, the private developer who under-

TABLE 3-2. *Use of Residential Acreage, Conventional Subdivision
and Clustering*

| Land use | Number of acres | |
| --- | --- | --- |
| | Normal subdivision | Cluster development |
| Housing | 84[a] | 42[b] |
| Open space and playground | 6 | 52 |
| Streets | 22 | 18 |
| Total | 112 | 112 |

Source: William H. Whyte, *The Last Landscape* (Doubleday, 1968), pp. 203, 204, 206.
a. 168 single houses on half an acre apiece.
b. 168 townhouses.

stands the land-saving potential of the cluster may use it to achieve greater density rather than a more spacious neighborhood.[24]

The relation of street space to traffic congestion is illuminated by the situation in the United States, where most cities of relatively high population density have a large proportion of their total area in streets yet suffer severe congestion. When this street area is related to population, however, the actual amount of street acreage per 10,000 persons is found to be low compared to that in cities which experienced most of their growth in the automobile era.

To illustrate, Phoenix, Arizona, has a low population density (2,343 persons a square mile) and uses a relatively small percentage of its area for streets (9.6 percent). But this small proportion of total land amounts to 341 acres for each 10,000 persons, nearly six times the figure for Cambridge, Massachusetts. Cambridge, with 17,098 persons a square mile, has 15.3 percent of its area in streets, but this is only 59 acres per 10,000 population. The result is heavy street congestion, even with a subway. An adequate system of transportation that will avoid congestion must take into account population density, per capita street area, the relative use to be made of automobiles and public transit, and the extent to which land-use arrangements are designed to reduce movement. Milton Keynes, for example, designed for no congestion, with 80 percent of all travel by car, allocates only 100 acres per 10,000 population to streets because it is designed to minimize home-to-work travel.

The concept of equating transport supply and demand is absent in the conventional city. Concern for balance is shown only for services that are absolutely vital to survival. Shortage of water, for example, is a

24. *The Last Landscape* (Doubleday, 1968), p. 212.

threat that cities move quickly to overcome. Nor are shortages of fuel, electricity, and telephone service tolerated for long in affluent societies. But all cities of the world put up with housing and transportation shortages. People can double up, sleep on the sidewalks, and stay home. An excess of transportation demand over supply can also be handled by tolerating congestion and dissipating the effects in unquantified social costs. The indifference of the unplanned community to embarrassing supply-demand relationships is exemplified by the zoning regulations of New York, which at one time made it legally permissible for 370 million people to live in the city. And until the mid-1950s, Chicago's zoning ordinance would have permitted everyone in the country to settle in Chicago.

The relative economy of planned and unplanned development is illustrated by proposals for a new city for 450,000 people on New York City's Staten Island. Here a 10,000-acre site known as South Richmond, the last open land in New York, is committed to a gridiron system of streets that will inevitably wind up with monotonous housing, little variety, and an absence of everything that could make the community pleasant to live in. The street system already developed or mapped will absorb 30 percent of the area.

If left to follow the trends, South Richmond would build 70,000 dwellings over the next thirty-five years for 250,000 more people, and the community would attract 40,000 jobs. The alternative is to plan the expansion of this area as a whole. Three possibilities were studied: a low-density city of 300,000 with 110,000 jobs; a medium-density city of 450,000 with 180,000 jobs; and a high-density city with a population of 675,000 and 250,000 jobs. Any one of the planned cities would offer far greater attractions than the disarranged conventional city. These include a new downtown center, convenient recreation, pedestrian walkway systems, partially self-contained neighborhoods with their own shopping areas and services, variety in housing, good facilities for industry, controls against blight, and a wide range of economic and social advantages.

All the new city proposals would require higher initial public investment—approximately $30 million a year—than the $10 million spent for development as now trending. But public investment per capita and per dwelling would be considerably lower for the planned communities: only $3,500 a dwelling but $6,200 for an unplanned community. This saving is due largely to more efficient use of the land. For example, for a medium-density planned city, only 16 percent of the land would be

used for streets, while 30 percent is now visualized as becoming necessary. Returns to the city on public investments would also be much
greater. Private investment opportunities in the planned cities are estimated to be three times as great as the economic activity attracted to
the unplanned community.[25]

Basing its proposal on the demonstration effect of planned communities throughout the world, the National Committee on Urban Growth
Policy has recommended that the United States construct 100 new
communities with an average population of 100,000 and 10 new cities
of a million people each to take care of 20 percent of the urban growth
anticipated by the year 2000.[26] According to the committee, "The European experience demonstrates that new communities can be, from the
beginning, places of openness and diversity. They can show just how
pleasant an urban environment can be."[27]

An opposing view contends that settling millions of people in new
towns is a policy unlikely to succeed. "There is little force in the arguments for a major national commitment of effort and resources to direct a substantial portion of our urbanization into new towns."[28] This
argument states that there might be grounds for experimenting with
new towns to test innovations for possible application to the expansion
and rehabilitation of existing cities. But as the University of California
report points out, badly needed are large-scale planned urban developments, in old cities and in future growth areas, that follow the example
of new town design to deal effectively with the interrelated needs of
urban residents and with the total environment.

It is in this total context that the lessons of the new cities should be
heeded. The new suburbs are going to be built, one way or another.
Their nature must be changed from the sprawling, monotonous, and
unattractive bedroom communities that so frequently mar the fringes
of the city to a combination of housing, work places, and recreational
areas that constitutes a partially self-contained organism in the larger

25. The Rouse Company, *A Report to the City of New York: An Analysis of Development Trends and Projections and Recommendations for a New City in South
Richmond* (Rouse, 1970), Chap. 2.

26. National Committee on Urban Growth Policy, *The New City* (Praeger for
Urban America, Inc., 1969), p. 172.

27. Ibid., p. 170.

28. William Alonso, "What Are New Towns For?" Working Paper 108 (Center
for Planning and Development Research, Institute of Urban and Regional Development, University of California at Berkeley, October 1969; processed), pp. 3, 39.

metropolis. Similarly, the urban redevelopment projects that have eradicated some of the blighted areas of the old city should not be replaced by a monolithic commercial development without residential areas, doomed to traffic jams in rush hours and to desertion at night and on weekends. Suburban developments and downtown urban renewal should be planned and carried out on a large scale as new cities meant to function as communities.

What the total planned community offers is the opportunity to complement new housing with recreation, schools, shopping, transportation, and other community services to serve the people who live in the housing, and to do so on a large enough scale to guarantee acceptable surroundings and accessible jobs. Land ownership and leasing arrangements under one management not only produce comprehensive design but also permit the increment in land value resulting from development to be used to help defray the cost of good housing and community facilities. The planned city provides the opportunity to design acceptable urban life systems.

# CHAPTER FOUR

# Applying New City Principles to Old Cities

Planned cities and urban redevelopment around the world demonstrate approaches to living and moving that can be applied in existing cities to arrest decay, restore vitality, and guide further growth. They involve not only ways of improving mobility and accessibility but also methods of making transportation contribute in a positive way to the quality of the urban environment. The cities already built cannot be abandoned, but in the process of maintaining, replacing, and expanding them it is possible to begin transforming them. Some important guidelines are emerging.

• The volume of movement in cities can be reduced substantially by making good housing and neighborhoods accessible to work places, and by assuring the proximity of residential areas to the daily needs of the household.

• Instead of focusing exclusively on transport solutions to urban congestion, intercity methods of transportation might serve more effectively to decongest the city by interconnecting many separate city centers in a polynucleated urban region.

• The location, design, and redesign of streets and other transportation infrastructure can help bring about new uses of land, reduce the pollution resulting from motorization, create new sites for housing, shopping, and industry, and enhance the appearance of the city.

• Walking is often the most efficient method of short-haul movement, and all communities should be supplied with facilities designed specifically for the pedestrian.

• Many types of urban futures will be wanted, ranging from the vertical high-density city to low-density suburbs and exurbias, but for all urban forms the achievement of efficient circulation and a livable environment will require a conscious matching of transportation capacity with the design and traffic-generating characteristics of the community.

Between the two extremes of urban living—the densely populated city centers, or communities without cars, and the dispersed pattern of rural life that depends on cars but dispenses with community—will be the extensive urbanized regions of many interconnected centers that will reconcile rural and urban as well as cities and cars.

*Transportation and Housing*

New cities and major urban redevelopment everywhere demonstrate the importance of creating a pleasant environment in which to house the urban population. In cities already built, large areas of land will have to be cleared if the housing backlog is to be reduced and neighborhoods with the necessary life support systems are to be built. Since conventional street patterns chop the urban area into small properties and allow motor traffic to intrude, major alterations to the street system will often be needed to make way for large-scale construction of housing. Transportation will have to supply access to new housing sites beyond the built-up area to accommodate families displaced by redevelopment and to meet the needs of population growth. Housing and transportation are closely related requirements, and each can help to achieve the simultaneous objectives of clearing the slums, creating attractive living conditions close in, and fostering the outward migration to planned communities.

In the teeming cities of the developing world, tens of millions are living under conditions of acute overcrowding, lack of sanitation, and often no housing at all. But even in high-income countries, including the United States, slums and blight are critical problems in spite of record levels of national prosperity. In many of Europe's industrial cities there are no adequate housing or neighborhood facilities for low- and middle-income workers, and in Tokyo and other Japanese cities housing has been so neglected that millions live in minimal space without private toilet or bath. The task of supplying decent homes and neighborhoods for the world's urban population will require not only massive rehabilitation of existing cities, but also an unprecedented effort to keep pace with growth by building planned urban settlements. Transportation now supplies the means of moving out into the space available and the technology to permit large-scale city-building without congestion.

In the United States the size of the housing backlog for low-income families is so great that a major obstacle is finding the land to build on. The Kaiser Committee report on urban housing measures the critical dimensions of the land acquisition problem. The committee concluded conservatively that 26 million new and rehabilitated housing units are needed in the next ten years to overcome the existing deficit and to provide for new growth, and that millions of acres will be required to

*A global problem: drab shelter in crowded surroundings*
Department of Housing and Urban Development

make this program possible.[1] Included in the total package would be 6 million subsidized units, or ten times more housing a year for low- and moderate-income families than has ever been attempted. This publicly aided program would absorb a minimum of a million acres for the housing alone, plus another million acres for recreation, shopping, industry, and other supporting activities. The 20 million unsubsidized homes in the proposed ten-year program would require at least 6 million acres more. Altogether, the 8 million acres of new urbanized land required in one decade constitute a 60 percent increase over any previous rate of land consumption for urbanization in the United States.[2]

The National Commission on Urban Problems has also documented the need for good housing sites to reduce the crowded conditions in central city slums and to make an accelerated housing effort possible.[3] Overcrowding in most central cities is denying recreation, pushing up the price of land, creating claustrophobia, and placing enormous burdens on transportation and public service of all kinds. With an expected urban population increase of 25 million a decade, it is not possible to alleviate overcrowding without substantial outward movement.

The highway and the motor vehicle together with good public transportation furnish the means of making new lands accessible for urban settlement. A planned dispersal of urbanization may ultimately be the most feasible answer to congestion, more practical than costly efforts to meet the needs of physically continuous urbanization.

Planning for new growth is especially important in the United States if a conscious effort is to be made to break up the racial ghettos. Providing planned communities for biracial living can offer an alternative to the folly of perpetuating a dual society. It must be decided whether a transportation strategy that would enable low-income workers to cover the distances to where there is work should be supported, or whether the preferable course would be to bring jobs and living closer together. The transportation costs of racial segregation are substantial. Many nonwhites must live close to the center away from job opportunities on the fringes, which in the future may constitute 80 percent of all the

1. *A Decent Home*, The Report of the President's Committee on Urban Housing (1969), pp. 3, 138.
2. *The Ill-Housed*, A Compendium of Recent Writings and Reports on National Housing Policy (Washington: Urban America, Inc., no date), p. 48.
3. *Building the American City*, Report of the National Commission on Urban Problems, H. Doc. 34, 91 Cong. 1 sess. (1969), p. 77.

new jobs available. At the same time white residents in suburbia travel longer distances to central business district offices than would be necessary in a nonsegregated urban society.[4]

Transportation has already led to better housing by opening up land that people can afford. By moving out, millions of families have been able to find better and more spacious accommodations and to put more money into the structure itself and less into the lot. For an average automobile commuting cost of $860 a year,[5] they can realize considerable saving in household costs over the more expensive close-in living, often with extra dividends in space and satisfaction.

But good living conditions need not be contingent on excessive costs of transportation and wasted time and effort in commuting. The present situation stems from the error of building housing developments instead of whole communities and thus separating the places where people live from the places where they work. The interstate highway system in the United States, for example, is being lined with modern industries at considerable distances from metropolitan centers with their housing and community facilities. The consequent daily commuting outward has overloaded the new transportation facilities, which in rush hours often resemble city streets. If these industrial developments were grouped together rather than strung out, and if housing and other facilities were planned to go with them, the result would be a new city with good housing and easy access to work instead of an unplanned environment with excessive commuting from inadequate housing. Highway and rapid transit programs should be combined with community building to develop new sites where suitable living and working conditions can be provided.

In the United States the construction of a national system of highways should have been combined with public acquisition of adjacent land where industrial and community development could have been accomplished at the same time. The highways then could have functioned as connectors between clusters, and much of the daily commuter problem could have been taken care of within the clusters. Instead, the

---

4. See "Race and the Urban Transportation Problem," Chapter 7 in John R. Meyer, John F. Kain, and Martin Wohl, *The Urban Transportation Problem* (Harvard University Press, 1966), pp. 144–67.

5. Average annual cost, total urban United States, 1966. U.S. Bureau of Labor Statistics, *City Worker's Family Budget for a Moderate Living Standard, Autumn 1966*, Bulletin 1570-1 (1967), p. 9.

highway system was permitted to induce an unplanned sprawl without compensating efforts to guide part of this growth into new communities. As a result, many miles of road were overloaded before the system could be completed. There is still ample opportunity, however, to use this long-distance transport network as a means of encouraging planned growth. Federal-state cooperation in land-use planning and in the acquisition of sites for development could guide the urbanization process and help focus the necessary investment in urban infrastructure.

The question that now arises is whether the new federal rapid transit and passenger railway programs for American cities are going to forgo a similar opportunity. Railway stations and bus terminals, like expressway interchanges, can be locations where new growth is planned for, encouraged, and organized. The global laboratory provides evidence that rapid transit built simply to relieve congestion will fail to do so, but such facilities built in conjunction with planned communities can be the means of gaining access to clusters that are congestion-free.

### Intercity Transport to Solve Urban Transport Problems

The use of high-speed intercity transportation may be one way to reduce the pressures creating congestion inside the cities. In France, for example, the number of people in the Paris region is expected to grow from 8.5 million to 14 million by the year 2000. Most of the growth will be absorbed by new satellite cities around the capital that will be connected by high-speed surface transport and expressways. And growth points have been selected throughout the country for the location of new industries, universities, and research establishments. These planned communities, made accessible by good transport, will increase the number of cities with 100,000 population from forty-nine in 1970 to eighty by the year 2000.

The Japanese, faced with the probability of 20 percent more people over the next twenty years (an increase of one million annually), also look to new satellite cities as a way out, and the first planned community for 450,000 is under construction twenty miles west of Tokyo. Land is being acquired for another about the same distance to the east, near the New Tokyo International Airport. High-speed rail connections will be built between the new settlements and central Tokyo. The practicability of semiconventional high-speed trains for regional transport under conditions of heavy traffic has been well demonstrated in Japan, where fully automated conventional trains with a sustained speed of 130 miles an hour and carrying capacity of 1,000 passengers a train make eighty trips a day in each direction over the 320-mile route between Tokyo and Osaka. The Japanese are planning a nationwide network of high-speed trains that could make the entire country function as one great metropolitan area.

Liverpool, England, is also developing satellite communities beyond its boundaries by purchasing land outside the urbanized area, with planning permission granted to it by the outlying governmental jurisdictions. These jurisdictions do the actual building of the new communities and are paid a flat sum annually for forty years to defray the cost of each citizen of Liverpool who leaves the city for the fringe area and helps the thinning-out process. The growth of Liverpool itself has been encouraged by the fast electric train service to Birmingham and London.

Innovations in transport now make it possible to bring together a complex of urban settlements, forming a polynucleated city. The association of urban communities of manageable size in an interrelated metropolis promises to achieve an environment better for humans. The trend toward lower costs and higher speeds of transportation, combined with telecommunications, presents a practical alternative to the solid build-up of the planless city. The regional city of well-defined clusters of activity, connected by rapid means of transport, can offer all the advantages of the big city without its ever-increasing economic and social costs.

As transportation opens up the countryside for urban settlement, the danger that desirable space will be overrun must be guarded against by general agreement on the boundaries of lands to be left in forest, farms, recreation areas, and useful open space. This involves decisions as to where city expansion is to be circumscribed, what land policies are required to keep cities from running into each other, what urban areas should be encouraged to expand, and what sites should have priority for future new communities. Setting national standards such as these should make it possible to divert the growth that focuses on a few overcrowded cities, dispersing future concentrations in a more balanced regional development.

A recent move in this direction is the proposal to pair nine redeveloped inner city areas in the Detroit metropolitan area with ten undeveloped areas in the suburbs, twenty to forty miles away, connecting the pairs by mass transit. New housing for a variety of income groups would be built in both inner and outer communities. The inner "new towns" would range in size from 600 acres to 2,000 acres and hold 25,000 people each, while the suburban sites would be considerably larger—up to 8,000 acres and 75,000 people. The proposed development would take place over a twenty-year period and cost $1 billion for each set of "paired towns." The idea, as in Singapore and Stockholm, is to give the central city a role in suburban development that will permit the redevelopment of the inner city and a socially acceptable diversity for the suburbs.[6]

*Transport Infrastructure and Urban Development*

Since a third of the world's population already lives in established cities, a primary task for transportation policy is to help in the redevelopment and reconditioning of the existing environment. The prospects for doing so are strengthened by the fact that so much of the urban area is absorbed by streets, and because, as many urban redevelopment projects reveal, street space can be effectively used to create new neighborhood patterns and more efficient organization of the community. Streets need to be relocated, rerouted, abandoned, and converted to create the framework for "new" cities in old cities. Urban roads, as the corridors and front parlors of the city, should be designed not only to travel on but also to live on. Street location and design can help reduce the effects of noise and pollution, and streets can be combined with other land uses and with buildings to become an integral part of the physical surroundings. Carrying out housing, shopping center, and industrial development projects depends in many cases on what is done with the streets in the way of large-scale rehabilitation over a sufficiently wide area.

The space devoted to streets usually represents the largest portion of publicly owned urban land. In the United States, where 25 to 30 percent of the city is streets, the combination of roadways and parking facilities in central areas may absorb more than half the available

6. See "Cities: Pairing the Old and New," *Time* (March 1, 1971), pp. 15–16. The plan was developed by Hubert Locke, Urban Studies Center, Wayne State University, for the Metropolitan Fund of Detroit. Each set of paired towns would be a social, economic, and political entity.

*Streets and parking—half the city*
Federal Highways Administration

space. These are the parts of the city most readily subject to public efforts to change the environment. They are also the areas seen and used the most, and their improvement, when combined with other projects, can accomplish major redevelopment.

New cities and urban redesign have demonstrated that transportation infrastructure is often successfully combined with park and recreation projects, housing, and commercial developments on a large tract of land. The highway can serve as the structural setting for such a development, its design and landscaping can enhance the whole area, and traffic problems can be alleviated at the same time.

There is a growing awareness of these potentials, and the results are visible in Stockholm's redevelopment, in London's housing estates, and in other redevelopment projects. In the United States, combining urban highway construction with neighborhood development has often been found to result in significant savings. Though building a road may call for acquiring only 40 percent of a block, this 40 percent often costs nearly as much as the entire block, because of the high payments for severance damages on partial takings. If the whole block is taken, the city may acquire the extra 60 percent of the block for only 20 percent more money.[7] The land adjoining the roadway can then be used for housing, play space, or a park.

Combining transportation with other development programs through the use of air rights over highways is also a means of supplying needed space at economical prices and overcoming the unwanted environmental effects of expressways. In 1968, thirty public or private projects were using the air space over federal highways, and another thirty-six such projects had been proposed. Most were private structures: stores, apartments, hotels, restaurants, parking areas, service stations, office buildings, schools, and residences. Public uses include housing, parks, schools, and public buildings.[8]

The use of air rights and motor vehicle tunnels can help to make the automobile unobtrusive, remove traffic and traffic noises from adjacent neighborhoods, and provide the additional advantage of parks and play-

7. David R. Levin, "Joint Use—Joint Development Concepts for Highway Corridors" (paper presented at the 54th annual meeting of the American Association of State Highway Officials, Dec. 4, 1968; processed).

8. U.S. Bureau of Public Roads, Environmental Development Division, "A Report on the Status of Multiple Use and Joint Development" (U.S. Department of Transportation, Federal Highway Administration, 1968; processed), pp. 8, 9.

grounds in the space above the depressed roadway. Because of the difficulty of driving in lengthy tunnels and because of ventilation costs, relatively short, unventilated tunnels that eliminate intersections are often the most effective means for reducing congestion and lessening the undesirable side effects of the automobile. Brussels has constructed a large number of these motor vehicle subways, and their use in Rome, Paris, and Washington illustrates their advantages. Ten miles of freeway in a city may cost $100 million, while the same amount could be used to eliminate the fifty busiest intersections at an average cost of perhaps $2 million. Selling the air rights could help pay the cost of the tunnel and create more pleasant surroundings.

The costs of landscaping, tunneling, and refining the design of expressways to improve environmental quality are substantial, but the developments made possible adjacent to a well-designed transportation facility can more than compensate for the extra cost. For example, the investment required to build an elevated expressway in New Orleans was estimated at $16 million, whereas putting the roadway on the surface would cost $29 million and a depressed roadway that would get the traffic entirely out of sight would cost $77 million. A study of the alternatives revealed that it would be preferable to build on the surface, at 75 percent more than the cost of the elevated structure, even though the surface route absorbed a substantial area of valuable riverfront property. What made the extra cost acceptable to the city was that the boulevard would permit a joint development of at least $100 million worth of structures adjacent to the highway.[9]

When a highway project is viewed as part of an areawide development, the least-cost solution from a transportation point of view is generally a very expensive solution from the standpoint of the community. Conversely, many cities have learned to take maximum advantage of a high-quality highway, and European cities in particular offer many good examples of how streets can make a positive contribution to the environment. The boulevards of Paris, Milan, Copenhagen, Turin, Lisbon, Madrid, and Barcelona give these cities character and beauty, and supply them with needed parks and attractive restaurants and shopping areas. Widths are frequently one hundred yards, but many roadways of lesser width are equally impressive. Along the lakefront in Geneva, the

9. Jeremiah D. O'Leary, Jr., "Evaluating the Environmental Impact of an Urban Expressway," *Traffic Quarterly* (July 1969), pp. 341–51.

Quai de Mont Blanc not only handles the movement of traffic but also satisfies the recreational needs of the area and adds to the aesthetic attraction of the neighborhood. Tree-lined sidewalks, lawns and flower gardens, sidewalk kiosks, restaurants, a marina and beach, together with adjacent hotels and apartments, make this right-of-way serve the combined purposes of transportation, housing, and recreation. The construction of such a boulevard was a means of filling many needs and enhances the whole city.

This use of lakefront space is in sharp contrast to the exclusive dedication of waterfront sites to highways. Along the Potomac in Washington, D.C., for example, the least-cost solution to moving traffic was the Whitehurst Freeway, an elevated highway designed only for transport, which took no account of the possibilities of using the waterfront for recreation and relaxation or of making the area available for housing, shops, and restaurants. Such a limited use of land highlights the need for new institutional arrangements that allow combining transport investments with private development as part of a total design for the environment.

Good examples of waterfront developments are Lake Michigan in Chicago, the waterfront transport and park systems in Havana, Hamburg, Manila, Rio de Janeiro, Copenhagen, Stockholm, and San Francisco, and river roads and parks on the Seine in Paris, the Tiber in Rome, and the Rhine in Heidelberg and Frankfurt. The potential has not been realized in Boston, Bangkok, Norfolk, Baltimore, Providence, Karachi, and other port cities with extensive waterfronts. All cities situated by water have the opportunity to combine transport with parks, housing, public buildings, and commercial development. But with single-minded devotion to moving traffic, many cities have turned their backs on the water and relegated it to ugly, nonproductive uses.

*Transportation and the Streetside Environment*

A distinguishing characteristic of streets in the motor age is the area given over to parked cars, billboards, signs, drive-ins, service stations, and other establishments that cater to the motorist. With utility poles and wires added to these eyesores, the street system that enables us to move has become a continuous slum that destroys the environment and discourages renewal.

*The living room of the poor*
Roland L. Freeman

At the first meeting of the Committee on Urban Housing, the President stated that the most pressing need in America was not only a decent home but healthy surroundings.[10] Reference to the surroundings is appropriate. It is not simply poor housing that creates physically run-down areas but the outlook from the house, the condition of the surrounding streets, and the uses made of them. What one sees in a slum neighborhood are broken and unmaintained pavements lined with cars that belong to someone else. The streets are important for transport only to those who use them to pass through or to park. The noise, dirt, and fumes of traffic have ruinous effects on adjacent housing and on the lives of those whose only meeting place and recreational area are the sidewalk and the street. Cleaning the streets and the streetsides and transforming their ugliness is a transportation problem that gets little if any attention. The United States can boast the most offensive streetscapes in the world, but the blight is rapidly spreading to other motorized countries. Doing something about it will not be "an acceptable substitute for dealing with the unsolved problems of housing, schools, and jobs. It must be seen as a first step."[11]

Hundreds of millions of dollars have been spent in the United States and elsewhere for landscaping highways in rural areas (where greenery is least needed), but rarely is this practice extended to the cities. Biologists tell us the time is ripe. Physically and genetically we are the product of millions of years of evolving in natural settings, and in our drab urban surroundings we still try to duplicate the tropical savanna by heating the air, growing plants, and keeping dogs, cats, and birds.[12] While the psychology of man's reaction to natural beauty, to the colors and sounds of nature, is still only faintly comprehended, the biological need for trees is now being met mainly by dead trees (poles), and those who long for green grass must put up with black asphalt.

A look at magazine advertising shows that a message to the public of what is best in any line invariably makes use of the elements of water, grass, trees, shrubs, and other greenery. Waterfronts, the most

10. A *Decent Home*, p. 1.

11. Kenneth B. Clark, "The Negro and the Urban Crisis," in Kermit Gordon (ed.), *Agenda for the Nation* (Brookings Institution, 1968), p. 137.

12. H. H. Iltis, P. Andrews, and O. L. Loucks, "Criteria for an Optimum Human Environment" (1967); cited by Paul R. Ehrlich, "Population," in *Man and His Environment: A View Toward Survival*, Major Background Papers, 13th National Conference of the U.S. National Commission for UNESCO, San Francisco, November 23–25, 1969 (U.S. National Commission, no date), p. 74.

common element in ads, are also the least available to the urban population. If advertisers are right, what the public likes and wants is either a completely natural environment or a high-quality man-made urban environment. That so many people are deprived of these backgrounds may account for the vicarious pleasure of seeing them in a magazine.[13]

In the United States, the President's 1965 State of the Union Message called for "a new and substantial effort . . . to landscape highways to provide places of relaxation and recreation wherever our roads run." The result has been partial control over outdoor advertising on 268,000 miles of main roads, regulations for control of junkyards, and special provisions for "landscaping and scenic enhancement."[14] The program has to a large extent failed for lack of funds and public support. Since 1965 money has been made available specifically for rural roadside landscaping, and the states have also been urged to spend regular construction funds for this purpose. Legislation or less formal procedures permit the purchase of land beside rural rights-of-way for scenic purposes, but this practice is not often extended to urban streets.

The cleanup that is bound to come must focus on commercial signs, which have contributed in a major way to the unsightliness of urban areas.[15] There are one million billboards on federal highways in the United States. The practice of destroying the roadsides in this manner is rapidly spreading in Europe and other parts of the world. If magazine advertising rates were charged for these encroachments, roadside advertisers would be paying several hundred times what they do now. A black and white page in *Life* magazine costs $36,500, a four-color page $54,000. Circulation is 8.5 million. A highway with 20,000 cars a day in one direction would have a potential readership (with 1.6 persons per car) of approximately 12 million a year. If total actual readership is assumed to be about the same for magazine and highway, yearly rates for billboards and similar advertising should average about $40,000 apiece. Where regulations fail, pricing policies might succeed.

Removal of utility wires and poles from the streets is also a key ele-

13. See Robert E. Coughlin and Karen A. Goldstein, Regional Science Research Institute, Discussion Paper 25 (October 1968), p. 30.

14. Highway Beautification Act of 1965, P.L. 89-285, Oct. 22, 1965.

15. To combat the present trends, Pittsburgh in 1968, under federal sponsorship, began testing a comprehensive graphics-and-color system for all types of street and direction signs, for various public facilities, and for commercial signs. Glenn Monigle, "Street Furniture and Shop Signs," in *The American City*, Vol. 83 (April 1968), pp. 99–100.

ment in making the transport network enhance the city. Europe leads the way in requiring underground installation of utility lines, and in all new cities the absence of wires and the presence of trees are striking characteristics of the new environment. As recently as 1955 installing underground wiring was ten times more costly than installing overhead wiring. The rate has been greatly reduced, partly because of the use of new synthetic materials for the installation and protection of lines and partly because of the reduced cost of trench digging. In the future the removal of overhead telephone and electric wires may best be accomplished by combining these utilities in accessible tunnels with other underground services such as water and gas lines and pipes for disposing of solid wastes. At the present time the burying of each utility in a separate and not easily accessible trench means that every repair and modification tears up the pavement and disrupts the movement of traffic. With a common utility trench serving piped and wired traffic of all kinds, and perhaps furnishing belt-line movement of freight as well, it would be possible by video surveillance to detect breakdowns and service interruptions, and to make repairs at minimum cost.[16]

Finally, properties along urban streets also play a major role in the total urban landscape, and the city must exercise controls that will eliminate abutting land uses that are unsightly. In rural areas control over the environment beyond the highway right-of-way is obtained by the purchase of scenic easements which prohibit property owners from using their land in ways detrimental to users of the road. Buying development rights prevents future structures from reducing or destroying the scenic nature of the area through which the road passes. The resulting "corridor management" on rural highways permits the New York State Thruway, for example, to control all development 1,000 feet back from the right-of-way on either side of 450 miles of the expressway. The practice ought to be adapted to the aesthetic requirements of city streets.

### Pedestrians and Aids to Walking

In new cities and urban renewal areas facilities for walking are a highly important part of the transportation system, and the advantages should be extended to cities generally, in whole downtown areas.

16. See University of Minnesota, Experimental City Project, *Minnesota Experimental City*, Vol. 2: *Economic and Physical Aspects* (The Project, 1969), pp. 4–5.

During the past half century the effort has been to adjust to the shift from walking to riding, as the average man for the first time has gained the technology and the affluence to make riding possible. But the growing conflict between man and machine clearly calls for recognition of the walker as an important subsystem of the transport network. Pedestrian walkways and shopping malls are now beginning to demonstrate the many desirable features of good pedestrian transportation that are applicable to all cities, new and old.[17]

Even in American cities with populations of one million or more, an average of 8 percent walk to work. In Boston and Pittsburgh one out of ten walks, and more than 20 percent walk in some of the smaller metropolitan areas. An additional number of employed persons work at home, thus reducing the proportion of the work force relying on the transportation system.[18]

A substantial volume of pedestrian traffic is also generated by the use of public transport. Walking to the bus is part of the system, and all subways in big cities seem designed to get the maximum pedestrian mileage. In addition, everyone is a pedestrian during his daily trips to stores, offices, and restaurants, making self-propulsion the principal short-haul method of movement. As Colin Buchanan, who directed the British Ministry of Transport study, *Traffic in Towns*, has pointed out, it is still possible for people to get around fairly well on foot when transit breaks down because of a power failure or a strike, "but imagine the effect on the city if walking should break down."

The trouble is that walking is breaking down, like public transit, because no one cares enough about it to make it work. The pedestrian is forced to use sidewalks that parallel the streets and maximize the fumes, noise, unsightliness, and danger. In the city, walking for pleasure is a contradiction.

The separation of pedestrians from motor systems accomplished in new cities can be achieved in existing cities by converting selected streets to pedestrian ways and barring automobile traffic during certain hours of the day. Permanent pedestrian ways can be built by installing pavements level with the curbs, then introducing lights, benches, landscap-

17. For a discussion of the functions of streets, see Jane Jacobs, *The Death and Life of Great American Cities: The Failure of Town Planning* (Random House, 1961), Chaps. 2–4.

18. U.S. Bureau of the Census, "Series III—Mode of Travel to Work" (special tabulation, no date), Tables 6A, 6D, 6G.

ing, and sculpture. Another possibility is the construction of more elaborate pedestrian plazas as part of an urban redevelopment project, with parking and transit underground.

Many European cities now provide streets exclusively for walkers; for example, Amsterdam, Cologne, Copenhagen, The Hague, Stockholm, and Barcelona.[19] Resulting crowds of shoppers have sharply increased retail sales for shops along the walkways. In addition to pedestrian streets and plazas, a number of cities are in the process of banning automobiles from large downtown areas. Vienna plans to reserve the city center inside the ring road for walkers. Essen and other German cities will have central pedestrian reservations more than a mile wide. Recently Rome removed the automobile from Piazza Navona. Florence followed suit with a ban on automobiles around its cathedral, and plans for carrying traffic under Trafalgar Square will give London a large pedestrian preserve where the person on foot can enjoy the full advantages of this historic area.

To date, however, there have been few attempts to ban the car from downtown areas altogether, although there are cities where vehicles are absent for economic or political reasons. Havana illustrates what a virtually carless city is like. "It has become above all a city to walk in," and with reduced traffic problems and air pollution, a city "to smell the sea in and watch the sky."[20] But the best model of a carless city is Venice, where complete freedom for the pedestrian offers useful ideas for application elsewhere. The main pedestrian island is three miles long and two miles wide. Residents and visitors leave their wheeled transport either at the railway station or in adjacent parking garages. From that point, the pedestrian uses the ninety-mile network of walkways, takes a water bus on main routes, or a water taxi that can operate on the 170 narrow canals and twenty-eight miles of lesser side canals. The transit system of 100 diesel-powered boats carries 70 million passengers a year. Venice may be a model for tomorrow's city. Its canals are like the depressed highways that will connect pedestrian islands or clusters of

19. More than 150 cities in sixteen countries plan or have effected the separation of cars from people. See C. Kenneth Orski, "Vehicle-free Zones in City Centers," Prepared for Presentation at the OECD Symposium on Techniques for Improving Urban Conditions by Restraints of Road Traffic, Cologne, Oct. 25–29, 1971 (Organisation for Economic Co-operation and Development, Environment Directorate; processed).

20. James Harvey, "The View from Cuba," *Commonweal*, Vol. 91 (Dec. 19, 1969), p. 353.

development in the polynucleated city. Extensive parking underground or on the fringes of urban clusters could create comparable areas of pedestrian safety, clean air, and quiet for conventional cities, with buses and taxis supplementing the walkways.

For existing cities the conversion of streets to walkways is best illustrated by Cologne. The widest parts of the black-and-white tiled walkways are approximately seventy feet across. The network is irregular with intersecting pedestrian streets adding to the variety. There are fountains, trees, attractive light standards, kiosks, and heated arcades off the main concourse. Buildings along the walkway are four stories high on the average, with shops and restaurants at ground level and living quarters above. Adjacent are high-rise apartments and public buildings.

The Cologne pedestrian network was at one time a series of ordinary streets for motor vehicles. The area was then closed to traffic and a new pavement installed to provide a level walking area. Vehicles are permitted to enter at specified hours to meet the essential transport needs of adjacent businesses. There are multiple-story parking garages nearby. Half the cost of repaving Cologne's pedestrian ways was paid by shopkeepers, but landscaping and lighting were financed by the city. All merchants objected to the pedestrian ways before they were built; afterwards all were in favor of them.[21]

Compared to the automobile, relatively little is known about the power, range, and operating costs of human beings, but it has been concluded that people refuse to walk more than 800 feet between parked car and destination and that the average nonstop trip distance on foot ranges from 400 to 600 feet per person. However, the same shopper may walk happily for much greater distances if the area is attractive. A random sample in Pittsburgh showed that out of a total of 135 pedestrian trips only 9 were longer than six blocks, whereas window shoppers on Fifth Avenue or the Champs Elysées may go a mile.[22]

21. See City of Norwich, City Hall, "Foot Streets in Four Cities: Dusseldorf, Essen, Cologne, Copenhagen," Report 3 (Norwich, England, November 1966; processed), p. 19. On the longest pedestrian street located in Copenhagen, for instance, 200 merchants conclude that benefits have been substantial, with sales up 30 to 40 percent the year following conversion. Sparks Street in Ottawa is another successful main street for pedestrians only.

22. Lester A. Hoel, "Pedestrian Travel Rates in Central Business Districts," *Traffic Engineering*, Vol. 38 (January 1968), pp. 10–13. Persons headed for restaurants generally moved about twice as fast as those whose destinations were retail stores, and travel by foot was faster in the morning hours than at midday and in cool temperatures than in warm.

Thus the future of pedestrianism will depend in part on the extent to which aids to walking can be introduced. Many European cities rent deck chairs or wooden chairs along walkways, on lawns, and in public squares. Most pedestrian streets have newspaper and periodical stands, commercial exhibits, and sidewalk cafés. Frequent restaurants or coffee bars provide an important psychological aid to walking, since those who venture forth on foot know there is a place to rest. Some cities protect pedestrians from the elements by arcaded sidewalks, as in Turin, making it possible to move about freely in rainy weather. Shopping arcades that pass through the interior of buildings also keep pedestrians out of the weather; an example is Milan's glass-covered Galleria with its shops and numerous eating places under cover. The arcades of Brussels are also inside shopping ways that may wind through, under, or over several buildings, making use of air rights where necessary.

New distribution systems, or people movers, will be needed to back up pedestrian systems. These can be operated in the core area of the business district, in building complexes, shopping centers, health and education centers, and large housing developments. If existing cities can be rearranged and redeveloped into clusters, transport systems built for short trips could include bicycle paths, moving sidewalks, electric cars, and minibuses.

The capacity of a moving sidewalk varies anywhere between 3,600 and 18,000 passengers an hour, with speeds limited to about two miles an hour for safety, although variable speed belts could achieve rates of up to fifteen miles an hour. The London Waterloo Underground line has a moving sidewalk, and one in the Paris Métro has a capacity of 10,000 passengers an hour in each direction. Another possibility is the rental of small, low-performance electric cars at parking areas, to be left at destination. Since distances in clusters would be short, electric car transport might be limited to an average speed of fifteen miles an hour and made available to persons of all ages as well as to the handicapped.[23]

The rising fortunes of the pedestrian are illustrated by the growing part of the urban transportation network that is going to be within buildings and in building complexes. New York City is introducing a new type of incentive zoning that promises to encourage pedestrian trans-

23. Clark Henderson and others, *Future Urban Transportation Systems: Descriptions, Evaluations, and Programs*, Final Report 1, Prepared for U.S. Department of Housing and Urban Development (Stanford Research Institute, 1968), pp. 22–25.

portation improvements by providing economic incentives that will persuade builders to introduce features the city is particularly anxious to have built, in return for zoning concessions that permit additional profit-making activities. Under the new zoning regulations, plans have been submitted for the construction of pedestrian crossings to neighboring buildings, underground pedestrian malls, and passageways to the subway. The incentive plan combined with the redesign of street systems could create the kind of internal circulatory systems needed to restore the pedestrian and separate people from motor vehicles.

### Matching Transportation with Urban Alternatives

New building complexes and entirely new cities are demonstrating that transportation infrastructure—the nontransport aspects of the transport system—provides the structural framework of the city, the most important element in city building. Problems of transportation are resolved not simply by how people move but by the character of the communities they move in: where things are located in relation to where people live and where they want to go.

Many different urban futures are feasible and can be made to suit many different life-styles and stages in the life cycle. There are also economic, demographic, cultural, and physical constraints that will necessarily lead to diversity in the nature of urban settlements. But in every case there must be a reasonably close match between the supply of transportation and the demand for movement. Any attempt to reach this balance by focusing exclusively on the supply of transportation will not only never succeed, but will destroy the environment in the process.

#### THE VERTICAL ENVIRONMENT: COMMUNITY WITHOUT CARS

Although the world's largest cities lack many of the agreeable things that people are seeking, they also offer advantages unobtainable elsewhere. An extensive program of new housing and neighborhood rehabilitation and the adoption of the best features of planned communities could help make the largest, most densely built metropolis livable. But the transport system will have to be primarily public transit if the capacity for movement is to be equal to the demand. This will mean control of automobile operation or exclusion of private cars altogether. It will also mean that central cities must be pleasant places to live in and not simply places to work in.

A variety of technological achievements is making mass transport megacities increasingly feasible. These include improved techniques for constructing higher buildings at lower costs, more efficient ways of excavating to provide underground space, and prospects for moving large numbers of people by subway. Other transport methods include high-speed elevators, escalator systems, moving belts, and someday automated highways and perhaps dual-mode mass transit technology that can accommodate both private cars and individual transit capsules. New transportation methods for long-distance movement—including jumbo jets, supersonic transports, giant cargo and container ships that require specialized ports, and high-capacity ground transport by rail or guideway—may also help big cities to flourish.

The trend toward high-rise construction has increased in recent years, and most large cities have established new records for building height. Factors behind the increase are the cost of land compared to the cost of buildings, and technological advances in construction materials. Cities could achieve considerably more vertical growth without detracting from the environment if the built-up area were planned to balance high-rise structures with appropriate transport systems. The Italian architect Paolo Soleri believes that vertical development is necessary for man to conserve energy, space, and other resources, and that the future lies in more dense and complex megacities.[24] We should combine architecture and ecology, he says, to produce vast, towering structures that reverse the present trend toward spreading out over the surface of the earth and concentrate several thousands or hundreds of thousands of people in a single giant building that will be the city of the future.

Soleri's proposed arcologies are several times higher than the tallest buildings in the world today, and rely on elevators, escalators, and moving walkways rather than space-consuming roads and cars. Automobiles would be stored in the basements of arcologies for use in interarcological transportation and trips to countryside destinations. Model arcologies already designed could house and serve a population three times the size of Manhattan's. Half a million people might live without crowding in a structure three-fifths of a mile high and a mile in diameter.

24. Paolo Soleri, *Arcology: The City in the Image of Man* (M.I.T. Press, 1969).

The importance of arcologies is that they would be able to make transportation an integral part of the community. Neighborhood levels would be linked to levels for stores, schools, industry, and recreation, with travel supplied by efficient internal transport systems. Commuting distances might be expressed in meters instead of miles, and people would be able to walk or ride bicycles. Inside the arcology there would be no need for cars. Public facilities, including universities, museums, hospitals, and concert halls, would all be located toward the center. The complex would be filled with parks and gardens, and residents would buy living space in large three-dimensional grids, using the space however they wished. The surrounding land would be open countryside, accessible without passing through miles of industrial zones and pollution. If world population is destined to rise to 20 or 30 billion one hundred years from now as predicted, then the megacity may be the only feasible home for man, and the automobile would have no relevance for intracity movement.[25]

The half-mile-high arcology is an exaggerated illustration of where urbanization in some cities seems to be heading. In Chicago one can live ninety floors up, commute sixty floors to work, and find all the necessary shops, services, and recreation in a single building. In many cities it is possible to live, work, and play in a complex of buildings in which transport is by elevator and pedestrian walkway and the automobile is left underground or on the periphery. In very high-density urban clusters, little room can be spared for automobiles on the surface, and the benefits to the few who can drive may be only a fraction of the social costs incurred by everyone else. For this reason the free transportation available within buildings and in clusters of buildings may need to be extended to wider areas of the city, not only reducing congestion but giving all urban residents equal opportunity to take advantage of what the city offers. In the world's high-density metropolitan areas the use of automobiles for travel from home to work in the center will be minimal, as it is already in London, Tokyo, New York, and Hong Kong. But the family car will still be desirable equipment for other operations, such as shopping, social and recreational travel, and transportation to suburban employment.

---

25. See Constantinos A. Doxiadis, *Ekistics: An Introduction to the Science of Human Settlements* (Hutchinson Publishing Group, 1968), p. 215. Even with effective birth control, the population of the world may be 12 billion by 2070.

SUBURBIA AND EXURBIA: CARS WITHOUT COMMUNITY

At the other extreme, more and more people are choosing to live an urban life without being physically located in a community. This has become possible through the use of the automobile and highway, the telephone and television, and soon the computer, because occupants of houses located in relative isolation or in isolated clusters have easy access to dispersed employment centers, schools, shopping, and recreation. This suburban and exurban living pattern, the major new dimension in urban America, competes as a way of life with conventional city and town. It is rapidly becoming popular in Western Europe, where suburban developments and modern shopping centers are suddenly duplicating the trends that have already made America predominantly a nation of urban low density. To a surprising degree the suburbs are spreading everywhere in the world. This type of living normally generates less traffic per mile than the capacity of the average road, and a favorable balance between transport supply and demand can be maintained by appropriate land-use planning. But unplanned dispersal for too many people can wind up creating a new kind of congestion caused by disorganization, with the result that traffic jams typical of the city are reenacted in the suburbs.

The dangers of dispersed and largely unplanned urbanization that transport now makes possible are revealed by current growth patterns in Connecticut, a state with the fourth highest population density in the United States. Approximately 85 percent of the 3 million people in Connecticut live in metropolitan areas, yet urban living consumes only about 9 percent of the land. A large number of families have one acre of land or more, and a major proportion of the new residential land to be used between now and 2000 will be for housing on lots of this size.[26] A survey of households in the state found that three out of four families prefer to live in a detached house and one out of three families wants an acre or more.[27] The fear of Connecticut planners is that if everyone has his way the features of the state that people most like will be destroyed. Residents interviewed said they liked best the appear-

26. Connecticut Interregional Planning Program, *Urban Development*, Connecticut: Choices for Action series (1966), p. 47.
27. Connecticut Interregional Planning Program, *Goals for Connecticut*, Connecticut: Choices for Action series (1966), p. 17.

ance of their surroundings; the second most desirable feature was good highways, which a dispersed population depends on to get to work and everywhere else. More than 98 percent of all trips in Connecticut are by road.

The problem faced by the state, therefore, is how to prevent the goals of mobility, dispersal, and good environment from becoming mutually exclusive. Regional planning officials have concluded that the solution requires a statewide land-use plan fostering a multiple urban center concept that would channel new growth into existing and new urban centers surrounded by reserved open space—"a pattern of related, but separate, urban islands."[28]

In countries where space is less abundant, there is even greater need for national and regional urban growth policies that channel urban growth in ways that preserve the environment and help to organize housing, community services, and work places. The need is for patterns of urbanization that provide partial self-containment, a mixture of rural and urban living, and areas of dispersal as well as concentration. These attributes are to be found in the regional city of many centers.

### THE REGIONAL CITY: CARS PLUS COMMUNITY

The automobile and the highway make possible a dispersed pattern of living, and the subway and rapid transit support the high-density metropolis. Both extremes are feasible, both have their following, and both can be made attractive or intolerable by the degree to which a conscious effort is made to solve their logistics. But for those who reject both high density and the absence of community, a third alternative with considerable attraction is the regional city, which combines urban densities with close-by country living. The regional city is made up of interconnected clusters surrounded by low-density land uses, where the special benefits of concentration can be enjoyed without succumbing to a continuous urban buildup unrelated to the countryside. The multicentered city offers a compromise between undesirably high density and the destructive side effects of indiscriminate sprawl. Stockholm and Singapore are multicentered regional cities.

The regional city promises to avoid the excessive concentration and

28. Connecticut Interregional Planning Program, *Choices for Action*, Connecticut: Choices for Action series (1966), p. 31.

size that destroy a sense of community by breaking up the continuous development of the metropolis, making cities manageable, and maintaining pleasant surroundings. An interconnected system of moderate-sized communities could create a sense of belonging and provide a basis for local self-government. At the same time scale economies could be realized through regionwide provision of transit, highways, sewage treatment, waterworks, and electric power. Regional cities of the future will combine the best aspects of both concentration and dispersal, as Lewis Mumford and others have visualized, in a setting that permits a closer relation between man and the natural environment.

The trouble is that in most parts of the world public policies and existing institutions are quite irrelevant to guiding urban growth and planning for the future city. A twofold challenge confronts urbanizing nations: the establishment of national policies to guide urban development according to preconceived spatial patterns, and the creation of city-building capabilities that allow community development and redevelopment on a scale large enough to transform the urban environment.

# CHAPTER FIVE

## Combining Transportation
## and Community Development

The jet age has led to the creation of a global laboratory in which geography has taken the place of history. We can now see for ourselves what cities were like before the automobile, how they functioned with mass transportation alone, what effects size and density have had on mobility, and how well transportation remedies now being proposed have actually worked. The exercise has undermined some popular assumptions.

The traffic jam, we discover, is present even where automobiles are absent.

Cities with the most public transit can suffer the worst congestion.

Making it easier to move often adds to the causes of crowding.

Systems of walking are frequently as important to the community as systems of riding.

Transport prevention through urban design may contribute more to mobility than increases in transport capacity.

Transportation, instead of having a negative impact on the environment, can actually improve it.

What these discoveries tell us is that many transportation solutions have little lasting effect in relieving urban traffic congestion, and conversely that transport can be used to create a new urban environment that rejects the crowding and chaos of the accidental city. Instead of merely coping with congestion, transportation combined with community planning can help rebuild existing cities without congestion, and it offers new alternatives for guiding urban growth.

Global experience also tells us how the new cities of the world are handling transport problems, and what lessons they offer for the redevelopment of existing cities. Listed below are features of the planned community that are relevant to the building of more satisfactory urban environments.

• Good housing close to employment to reduce average home-to-work travel distance.

• Industrial estates that make good neighbors.

• Community facilities convenient to housing to reduce repetitive daily trips.

• Underground freight delivery at major shopping and neighborhood centers.

• High-quality public transit serving all areas of the community, with low fares or no fares.

• Major highways and transit services designed to connect clusters of development.

• Pedestrian-oriented clusters with circulation systems of elevators, escalators, moving sidewalks, electric cars, minibuses, and underground terminals and parking.

• Public land acquisition to permit large-scale development and eventual recoupment from increased land values to help finance low-cost housing and community services.

• Preservation of open space or low-density land uses surrounding cities to prevent continuous urbanization and pollution of the land.

• Community designs aimed at reducing not only the percentage of urban areas devoted to streets, but also per capita local travel requirements and the proportion of urban resources allocated to transportation.

• Landscaping of the streets and control of commercial encroachments.

These features can be incorporated in a wide variety of urban designs to meet many different life styles, personal tastes, and economic or geographic constraints. Both the high-density vertical city and dispersed exurban living can be supported if public policy ensures a practical degree of integration between the community and its transportation.

*A Program for Transportation and the Environment*
*in the United States*

The major obstacles to a satisfying urban environment for Americans in an automotive age are institutional obsolescence and the lack of a national commitment to create pleasant cities and to establish the necessary priorities for urban reconstruction and development. Yet many of the concepts and tools are available, as well as the necessary resources to get started. Useful experience has been gained from the Model Cities program, which focuses on the social needs of community renewal, including programs for health, education, job training, recreation, day care centers, and other social services. The housing aspects of a total approach are being furthered by federally sponsored efforts to apply industrial techniques to home building. Operation Breakthrough is the beginning of a shift from conventional housing construction to mass production. It has been frustrated by the hostility of suburban residents toward having low-income neighbors and by the resistance of the building trades and local code authorities to changes in construction techniques and materials. But the building of new communities in jurisdictions less affected by conventional restraints may soon provide a setting for the promised breakthrough.

The success of these and other urban programs might be substantially furthered by an urban transportation program that would inject a large amount of capital to improve public transportation, to redesign the streets, and to promote community developments reconciling the automobile and the city. In the United States during the 1970s an estimated quarter of a trillion dollars will be spent in the public sector for transportation. A major source of this money is the $16 billion of revenue collected annually from motor vehicle taxes. About $5.5 billion of this is federal taxes now being deposited in the Highway Trust Fund, a large part of which is used for construction of the interstate highway system. That program is winding down, a surplus is building up, and over $6 billion a year (at current tax rates) will be accumulating in the fund. Some of this will be needed for continuing programs on primary and secondary federal aid roads, but at least half of the money will be available for new programs. It is time to use these funds to help solve the problems of urban areas.

Such a shift would mean a major transformation of the highway program. Building rural roads is relatively straightforward, whereas providing transport capacity in cities is often extremely complicated. A program most helpful to the city may not be more roads or even public transit alternatives, but rather good housing and pleasant neighborhoods near employment opportunities and community facilities.

Transportation resources can help make these changes possible. Funds to accommodate the automobile should not be used exclusively for highways; they should be spent for the creation of a total system in which the automobile can be useful without being destructive. This can be accomplished only through a combination of transport, urban redevelopment, and community design. Hence, the original idea of a highway trust fund is obsolete, and a transportation trust fund would not go far enough. What is needed is a fund for urban transportation and the environment.

Special fund financing, if it is to be continued, should be made responsive to the total needs of the city: alternative high-quality public transit, relocation and redesign of the streets, landscaping, building pedestrian ways, and forming sites for shopping, industry parks, and housing, designed for access by automobile. Motor vehicle funds should be combined with other urban programs to help create planned communities that respond to the needs of a motorized society.

An institutional arrangement for combining urban development and transportation investments has already been established in the New York State Urban Development Corporation, the purpose of which is the construction and reconstruction of cities. Recent federal legislation provides financial support for this approach through the Community Development Corporation within the Department of Housing and Urban Development. In addition, the Federal-Aid Highway Act of 1970 authorizes the secretary of transportation to use money from the Highway Trust Fund to make grants to states for primary highways to designated economic growth centers, planned for populations of up to 100,000 and designed to attract industry. If these programs of the Department of Transportation (DOT) and the Department of Housing and Urban Development (HUD) were combined, together they could supply all the ingredients for large-scale redevelopment and new city building: transportation, land acquisition, housing, community facilities, and economic development, together with center city slum clearance and renewal.

Such a partnership between HUD and DOT (carried out by private community builders) suggests as a first step that federal aid be made contingent on the creation of state urban development corporations, which would be the recipients of major federal grants affecting urban redevelopment and new communities. State highway departments, private housing construction firms, and other existing public and private agencies would participate in various aspects of the work, as is the case for planned community development in other parts of the world.

The precise nature of how transportation outlays might be used to support new city building and urban redevelopment would depend on specific community plans, but a sample program is presented in Table 5-1 to indicate the scope of the effort. The program would allow conversion of streets in existing cities to make them contribute to a quality

TABLE 5-1. *A Sample Ten-Year Program for U.S. Urban Transportation and Environment*[a]

| Purpose | Units affected | Unit cost (millions of dollars) | Ten-year cost (billions of dollars) |
|---|---|---|---|
| Making cars unobtrusive, by underpasses, tunnels, and use of air rights | 2,500 locations | 4.0 | 10 |
| Converting streets to pedestrian ways, parks, playgrounds | 10,000 miles | 0.2 | 2 |
| Construction of boulevards in central cities | 500 miles | 10.0 | 5 |
| Construction of off-street parking areas | 10,000 areas | 0.1 | 1 |
| Improvements in public transit networks | Cities of over 50,000 population | — | 20[b] |
| Removal of streetside utilities, construction of utility trenches | 100,000 miles | 0.05 | 5 |
| Elimination of commercial strips, landscaping of streetsides | 100,000 miles | 0.02 | 2 |
| Providing street systems for planned communities | 300 sites | 50.0 | 15 |
| Total cost | | | 60 |

a. To be carried out through state urban development corporations with the participation of state departments of transportation.
b. Includes $10 billion from federal transit program and $10 billion from motor vehicle taxes.

urban environment, and would provide the roads, parking, and public transit necessary to supply mobility for all residents in both old cities and new. It would also authorize land acquisition adjacent to highways for new housing, recreation, shopping, and industrial park developments. Transport solutions would in turn be aided by community design, including the location of housing and employment opportunities, shopping and services, and other factors governing the generation of traffic.

In ten years a combined federal and state urban transportation effort, with 70 percent of the money coming from the federal trust fund and

30 percent from the states, could make available at least $50 billion, in addition to the $10 billion provided by the federal government for mass transit. This $60 billion program could help support a combined attack on slums, housing deficiencies, and congestion and would provide major job opportunities for center city residents now encountering high rates of unemployment.

For America, the importance of a combined program of urban redevelopment and new communities goes far beyond decongestion and a quality environment. If a dual society of black cities and white suburbs is to be averted, there must be new housing and prospects for a better life in the central city for all, and for blacks, freedom to move into suburban communities. Such a strategy will depend to an important degree on a simultaneous physical upgrading of the central city and construction of attractive planned urban satellites.

### Urban Transportation Policy in Europe

Many of the policies recommended for immediate and long-term implementation in the United States are relevant to other developed countries, including those in Europe. But Europe's confrontation with the automobile is different in important respects. The historic value of the old cities has discouraged tearing things down to make way for expressways and parking lots, the centers still maintain a good balance of living and working, and there is less urban decay and abandonment. Europe has maintained an attractive central city environment, its public transit is generally satisfactory, and high densities continue to supply the transit systems with high levels of patronage.

But traffic congestion in European cities is at a near-crisis stage, with the full force of the automotive revolution still to come. More car ownership and more migration from agriculture to urban-industrial life can be expected with the trend toward greater affluence and the introduction of new scientific methods in agriculture. Urban traffic jams that are already near absolute limits in the largest cities must be expected to grow worse, without much chance of expressway, parking, and redevelopment solutions on the scale that is possible in America.

The maintenance of good public transit and commuter rail service in Europe, therefore, and the current expansion of subway systems are important alternatives to the automobile for commuter trips, and these may serve to slow the retreat from central cities. The conversion of streets to pedestrian systems, along with the exclusion of motor traffic from limited areas of historic importance, will also help.

Still the outward movement in search of more space will accelerate. Europe has a large number of attractive small and moderate-sized cities and towns, and thanks to the automobile and other transport, and to communications technology, these potential growth points are now within convenient distance of the metropolis. One possibility for de-congesting the big city will be to encourage the growth of these smaller cities. Europe's pioneering in the building of new communities increases the prospects for building more and for grafting onto existing cities the necessary planned additions. These can be designed with major reliance on the automobile for local movement and on good rapid transit for long-distance commuting.

European countries also enjoy the advantage of having pioneered in new institutional arrangements for the provision of urban transportation and for combining transportation investments in total community plans. They are not hampered as much by rigidities in the use of highway funds, and they are accustomed to municipal ownership of land and to the use of revenues from increased land values for public purposes.

The British appear to be closest to an organizational arrangement for relating transport to urban plans and for integrating various types of transport into a single system. Since January 1970 the Greater London Council, encompassing a 600-square-mile area and a population of 8 million, has had the task of transport planning for the London area as well as of overall planning. The London Transport Executive, which was created in 1970 to own and operate the subway and bus systems, is subject to the policies established by the council. The council is responsible for the Greater London Plan, and while detailed planning is assigned to local governments, the latter must adhere to the general framework of the comprehensive plan. The Greater London Council also has the power to establish a great variety of detailed traffic engineering remedies throughout the area, in consultation with the local boroughs. These include street parking controls, off-street parking facilities, traffic signal systems, and one-way streets. In addition, the council is responsible for major roads, railway policy, bus investments, transportation financing, rates, and subsidy policies. A Greater London Transport Group, which includes representatives of the council and the railways and public transit officials, formulates transport plans and facilitates projects affecting two or more jurisdictions or transport methods.

The city-building and renewal programs of Stockholm also illustrate the increasingly effective arrangements being developed to integrate land and housing policy as well as street and public transit operations. An important ingredient of Swedish urban development has been the policy of purchasing land within and outside the city at an early stage to guide urban growth and to reap part of the financial rewards from the resulting increment in land value. Public ownership of urban land has permitted the municipality, rather than the land owner and real estate developer, to benefit from the urbanization process, and this has been an important measure for avoiding the financial difficulties that confront so many cities around the world.

In most of Europe the land available for a dispersed pattern of living is limited, but increases in agricultural productivity are continuing to add to the available space, and with appropriate safeguards there could be considerable relaxation of the generally severe restraints now imposed on the use of open land. Without such relaxation, the automobile and the highway cannot be successfully used to decongest the old cities and increase available living space. For the automobile is to a large extent barred from big city centers by physical constraints and will find effective use only in the low-density areas now being developed and in the new regional city of many centers. A compelling need will be to plan the use of all the land to avoid pollution of the environment by uncontrolled sprawl, to preserve or restore the quality of life in the old centers, and to guide urban expansion into new communities or existing small cities that can be designed to absorb new growth without sacrificing their unique quality.

Europe's housing needs suggest that here, as in the United States, major efforts should be aimed at replacing obsolete structures and inadequate neighborhoods as well as at providing for growth. The combination of new housing and industrial and institutional construction will accelerate the dispersal of urban settlements and the creation of satellites around existing metropolitan centers. These will be facilitated by the well-developed networks of intercity transport railways and by advances in tracked air cushion vehicles and other high-speed ground transportation methods. Public transit to supplement the automobile will continue to provide access to a diversity of urban living. The ancient city centers may rely exclusively on good public transport, with strict controls on the automobile; smaller communities will be connected by rail to the big cities but will depend mostly on car and bus; and there will be large areas of dispersed low-density living that are completely motorized.

European patterns will not be fundamentally different from those of the United States, but greater physical constraints on the use of automobiles and more opportunity to learn from experience could minimize the repetition of America's worst mistakes: the abandonment of the center city, the uncontrolled commercialization of urban roadsides, the neglect of public transport, the absence of community planning, and lack of concern for the environment.

## The Developing Countries: National Urbanization Planning

In developing countries the automobile's invasion of the cities and the migration from farm to city resulting from the agricultural revolution have just begun. The extreme congestion that already afflicts most of the principal cities of Asia, Africa, and Latin America makes it difficult to visualize how matters could get much worse. But they are bound to, as the combination of more people and more cars adds to the paralysis of the big city.

The dilemma of the developing countries is that the big city, with all its problems, is also the means of achieving economic and social progress. Countries with the highest rate of urbanization have the greatest life expectancy, the highest literacy, the largest school enrollment, the largest newspaper circulation, the most favorable ratio of doctors to population, the highest calorie and protein intake, and the highest per capita income.[1] The trouble is not with urban centers as a way of life, but rather with the nature of urban growth and the lack of effort to capitalize on urbanization as a growth factor. Urban expansion needs to be encouraged in ways that will avoid unnecessary costs and create maximum development.

Developing countries need a plan of deliberate urbanization to accelerate the urban growth process and make it a positive force for development. The attack on subsistence agriculture ought to be duplicated by attacking subsistence urbanization in which social costs are high and productivity far below what is possible. In developing countries the planless expansion of one or two cities affects a sizable percentage of

1. United Nations, *Urbanization: Development Policies and Planning, International Social Development Review*, No. 1 (1968), pp. 21–35.

*Designed for living: Columbia, Maryland*
The Rouse Company

*Restored for living: Philadelphia*
Lawrence S. Williams

*Designed for shopping: Fresno, California*
Tidyman Studios

*Designed for playing: New York City*
David Hirsch

the total urban population, overcrowding reaches critical proportions, and the cost of effective remedies becomes prohibitive. These cities serve as magnets that continue to attract people from smaller towns and rural areas. Transportation generally strengthens this magnetic power through investments in ports, airports, rail terminals, and other infrastructure that concentrate industry and markets, while it could divert traffic from already overcrowded cities and create new activity centers of more moderate size.

Developing countries might move more rapidly from the preindustrial, or transitional, stage into the industrial or even the mass consumption era by concentrating on productive cities as they have on productive farms. Following the green revolution that is modernizing agriculture, the gray revolution that is urbanizing large areas of the developing world should be creating acceptable destinations for those leaving the farms and villages. It is essential to begin now to focus investments that are going to take place anyway—in housing, education, and industrial development—to create new growth points and to reinforce existing moderate-sized cities.

Transportation and communications to make possible a wider distribution of urban centers have arrived at just the right time. Not only is population growth making concentration in a small number of large cities totally unrealistic, but at the other end of the spectrum scientific agriculture is demanding a network of market towns to provide the farm with necessary agricultural supplies and the farmer with outlets where his produce can be sold, stored, processed, collected, and reshipped. The creation of major growth points for agro-based industries and other industrial plants that require plentiful space could lead to attractive cities that would exercise a restraint on migration to the metropolis. This might be achieved by allocating public resources for development to selected medium-sized and growing communities considered to have the best promise of becoming important larger cities. Highways, motor vehicles, and air transport services aimed at encouraging such development patterns, along with radio, television, and telephone, would be powerful tools to aid this effort.

A program of city building along these lines is an indispensable part of improving present conditions in grossly overcrowded capitals, for improvements in big cities will tend to increase their drawing power unless comparable measures are taken elsewhere to create genuine alternatives. What is needed, therefore, is a national view of the urban problem, and the use of transportation and other programs to create preconceived urban patterns.

The developing countries have several advantages in this undertaking. Many are just beginning to build their main systems of modern roads, and they have the additional opportunity of focusing the many other infrastructure investments only now becoming possible as national incomes rise. These facts and the relatively early stage of urbanization mean that there is still considerable flexibility in charting the course of future development. There is much to be gained by doing what is necessary to avoid unmanageable cities. An overgrown and inefficient city, like an obsolete factory, can mean a drag on industrial development and added difficulty in competing for world markets.

In developing countries, then, the impending collision between growing cities and increasing numbers of automobiles is not likely to be resolved short of a concerted effort to provide good public transport and to plan communities so as to minimize transportation and distribute urban concentrations more widely. Most of the measures for immediate relief cited earlier for application in the more developed cities of the world are also relevant to Calcutta, Karachi, and Manila: charging the motorist for the social costs and peak-hour costs of city driving, restricting street parking, introducing modern traffic-control systems, and furnishing high-quality, low-fare public transportation, including bus service on exclusive rights-of-way.

A basic question is whether or to what extent the automobile should be barred from some city centers altogether, on the grounds that very high densities preclude efficient automobile use and that a very small percentage of the population can be automobile owners in any case. In some large and densely populated cities the decision to ban automobiles could result in savings in transport costs sufficient to finance a high standard of free bus transit.

In large cities of the developing world, therefore, the economic and social effects of the automobile can be viewed in two different ways. From a negative point of view the automobile represents a very substantial drain on limited resources and is often a heavy user of foreign exchange. It can be purchased by only a relatively small percentage of the population, and therefore intensifies the inequality among income classes. Yet even the few who can afford an automobile create severe congestion on the streets of the city and slow the movement of trucks and buses.

The magnitude of the resources commanded by the automobile is indicated by estimates that, if current trends persist, over the next twenty years a total of $100 billion may be spent for the purchase of motor vehicles in seven Southeast Asian countries. This sum does not include the cost of operation or of highways. Expanding automobile use will at the same time create strong pressure for rapid transit solutions to combat traffic congestion on surface streets. Subway systems are extremely expensive, and instead of decongesting the city, they may encourage crowding and create a new imbalance between transport supply and demand at a higher level of intensity. A subway will shift public transit from buses to underground rail, but the space vacated by the bus will, in the absence of controls, be absorbed by more automobiles, so that congestion will continue unabated. Transit patrons, most of whom use bus lines at one or both ends of the subway ride, are still subject to surface traffic, and low-income residents, whose transportation needs are generally short trips for a variety of household purposes, may not find it convenient or economical to use the subway. Meanwhile, the high cost of a limited mileage in underground facilities is added to the expense of maintaining streets and motor vehicles.

Under these circumstances a developing country might well decide to exclude the private car from the central city, design the existing street system for the more efficient use of buses, and thus postpone or avoid investment in subway rapid transit as well as reduce the demand for roads. Resources can then be diverted from transportation to housing and other needed community services. By locating housing convenient to work places, part of the commuting problem can be overcome by minimizing transport.

On the other hand, the economic activity and employment created by the automobile are often significant, especially where motorization is supported by indigenous materials and production. Doing without the automobile may mean doing without a great many other things as well —the economic support industries, the economic incentives of car ownership, and the social effects of greater mobility. The question of what public policy to adopt depends on the degree of development and of resource endowment, as well as on the nature of the urban setting.

### Stages in Urban Mobility

Resolving the dilemma posed by the automobile and the city depends on the economic circumstances in which the problem arises. Four stages can be identified. First is an early period of low income, when car owner-ship is limited to a few high-income users, and the broader economic and social effects of the automobile are negative. Second is the stage of economic takeoff and expanded car ownership, in which each feeds on the other. The third stage is one of high levels of car ownership, when automobiles create congestion that reduces the effectiveness of both the city and the car and induces the search for rapid transit substitutes. A fourth and later stage emerges when the failure of mechanical trans-port solutions and the deteriorating environment focus attention on the underlying need for planned communities.

In low-income countries the first stage is heavily weighted by pedes-trian and bicycle movement, with varying degrees of reliance on bus or commuter railway. In such countries the automobile is used only by the rich and by officials. At this stage the automobile is indeed the insolent chariot, disregardful both of the nonmotoring public and of economic exigencies. The poor cannot afford cars, yet at some later stage in the growth process the automobile revolution gets under way and is closely associated with rising economic activity. Before cars are excluded be-cause a country is poor, it is important to know whether, to what extent, or at what time the automobile may help to promote economic growth.

The arguments that the automobile is a luxury and interferes with development have some substance, but they are not new and they are not wholly convincing. Sixty years ago in the United States the an-nouncement by Henry Ford that he would produce a million cars pro-voked the criticism that not that many people could afford a car, and that in any event the country could not afford the roads. The same position was taken in 1956 when the Japanese were debating whether to diversify from a rail and water economy to motor transport. Those op-posed to the automobile said that the country was too poor, there was no fuel, petroleum and other imports would create a serious drain on foreign exchange, and in any event the road system was not designed for motor vehicles. But when per capita income reached $250, the Jap-anese automotive revolution began, and within a decade and a half the land of the ricksha had 20 million motor vehicles, an extensive petro-leum-refining capacity, a nationwide system of good roads, and a spec-tacular economic growth rate that seems to have been sustained to no small degree by economic activities supporting the automobile.

In Europe the automobile revolution was interrupted by the Second World War. But by 1950 recovery had pushed per capita income above the $450 level, and the creation of jobs and new industries resulting from the growth of car ownership played a key role in further accelerating the economic and social revolution in Europe.

The evidence suggests that whereas in early stages of economic growth the private car can be a negative factor in development, especially where there are no automotive support industries, at a later stage the automotive revolution triggers economic and social change. Automobiles and the desire for automobiles become promoters of direct and indirect economic activities, and the new mobility begins to induce important changes in attitudes and horizons.

To hasten this second stage in developing countries, the suggestion has been made that automobile production be regionally organized on an international basis to promote specialization and scale economies. This could be accomplished by manufacturing a rugged low-cost vehicle that might serve the same purpose as the early Model T Ford, which was the primary means of getting America out of the mud and of bringing rural people into contact with urban life. The modern counterpart of the Model T would be equipped to cut wood, pump water, and thresh wheat. To achieve an integrated international production system, all countries would share in the production of parts and accessories. The output and employment engendered might have important effects on development, and a widely available low-cost vehicle might have favorable social and political implications.

Much of the world is now in the third stage, when congestion makes movement in the city difficult and the urban environment becomes increasingly objectionable. Subway and rapid transit systems are commanding renewed attention and greater resources, and moves are being made to give priority to transit in the use of surface streets and expressways. In many high-density center cities the subway seems essential at this stage. But lacking control over automobile use and over the density and arrangements of development, cities quickly discover that subways are no panacea for their problems.

Even as the world's cities are resorting to new mass transport solutions, the fourth stage in urban transportation is beginning to emerge. This is the stage when all solutions to urban transportation problems become suspect, and municipal officials begin to turn instead to urban design and ways of bringing about a better balance between transportation supply and demand. Stage four solutions will involve a combination of technological advances affecting transport (transit innovations, automobile guidance systems, and new power sources) and changes in the design of communities (cities that substitute planned activity systems for travel, and good housing and environment for the desire to escape).

The fourth stage will be decisive. The guiding principle will be to minimize unnecessary movement, to control the automobile to safeguard the urban environment, to invent acceptable substitutes for the automobile, and to meet the transport needs of the nondriving population. Developing countries have an opportunity to reduce the costly effects of stages two and three by moving as quickly as possible into stage four.

Universally called for in the fourth stage is a new focus on the basic needs of the urban poor. The enormous tasks of housing and slum clearance and the mounting pressures for water and sanitation imposed by urban growth make it highly dubious to concentrate resources on transportation. A solution is to deal with fundamental problems, using urban design techniques that minimize the repetitive daily trips generated by the disarrangement of the accidental city. In this way the major priorities for an improved environment to live in are given attention while many of the transport requirements of the urban area are being resolved as an extra dividend.

The need to minimize unnecessary transportation costs through planned city building and renewal is a principle illustrated by the debate over an adequate medical system for the United States. It has been pointed out that one solution to the health problem is not more doctors and hospitals, but less demand for treatment. This would be accomplished by preventive measures: a change in diet and life-styles, more exercise, fewer bad habits, and a consequent reduction in the need for medical attention. With the nation's health bill already close to $75 billion annually, the principal need is for a health strategy that produces better results for less money and permits the savings to be allocated to the creation of a healthy environment.

The case for preventive transportation is much the same. Spending for transportation has become a bottomless pit. In the United States the total annual transport bill is about $190 billion. But spending more money for moving is no guarantee that the traffic will move. The underlying reasons for today's congestion are the disarrangement of the city and the blighted conditions of the urban environment. Cities are investing too much in transportation to compensate for investing too little in everything else.

*Telecommunications and Life-Styles*

A strategy for reducing waste motion starts with urban design, but it will be reinforced by new technology in communications. The wired city of the future will have two-way telecommunications and a tie-in to computerized information that will enable urban residents to dial for many services now obtainable only by making a trip. Cable systems will make multiple channels available for a great variety of daily services at low cost, and two-way interactive systems will permit new methods of education and changing patterns of employment location, work habits, and recreation.

The significance of communications as a substitute for transport derives from the fact that while the unit costs of transportation continue to rise as quality declines, telecommunications tend to increase in quality and decline in cost. Distance is important in transportation, but with communication satellites distance is almost irrelevant. The question is how many of the functions for which transportation is now used can be performed by a picture telephone, a computer console, or a closed-circuit television system. Obviously, many trips can be satisfied by communications, and many others cannot.

For certain types of entertainment it is already clear how far television has gone in reducing evening trips to movies, concerts, plays, and other forms of leisure-time activity. Even shopping trips, which now account for a considerable percentage of urban travel, may be reduced by improved communications that include television displays, telephone orders, and automatic billing. The work trip, however, offers the greatest potential for relieving congestion by substituting communications. Already it is possible for widely dispersed participants to conduct joint operations with the use of computers, and opportunities to conduct many kinds of work (research, insurance, banking, editing, typing) at locations away from congested central business districts will increase. Since about two out of five of the urban trips made all over the world are going to work and returning home, the possibilities of reducing peak-hour traffic by changing the relation between home and work places are tremendous.

The advances in communications come at a time when the majority of workers in the more developed countries are in service industries that can benefit most from them. In many of these activities, jobs can be expected to become more task-oriented than time-oriented. Not all employees will work in an established office at an established time, offices will not have to be centrally located, and commutation may not have to be concentrated in the rush hours.

Offices in the future may provide suburban branches for the convenience of employees who can work together effectively with picturephones and time-sharing computer systems. There may be new home designs to isolate working members, and neighborhood office space within walking distance. Reports and correspondence will be transmitted between offices as readily as a telephone call, and computers will edit, correct, illustrate, and make cooperation among widely separated participants possible. It will also be possible to query libraries and other information sources to obtain needed material via printed form, voice, or illustration. "Hopefully in the future we will be able to live where we like, travel chiefly for pleasure, and communicate to work."[2]

The national investment required to wire half of the 100 million homes in the United States expected by 1980 is estimated to be $5 billion, less than 10 percent of the cost of the 42,500-mile interstate highway system. The cost of extending cable systems to homes in scattered locations and low-density areas would be prohibitive, but microwave relays and satellite systems will provide low-cost means of including these nonurban homes.[3]

The postindustrial city will become more accessible, then, as communications make for less commuting and less congestion. The peak-hour problem may partly take care of itself by an absolute reduction in demand as well as by more staggering of hours and days of work. Proportionately more travel may be for education and recreation, and vacation trips may be distributed more evenly around the year. Community design combined with changing life-styles could prove to be the important breakthrough in the effort to cope with congestion.

### The Coming Era of City Building

The conflict between the city and the car and the absence of satisfactory mass transit solutions stem largely from the fact that problems of transportation have been viewed too narrowly to permit the kind of

2. John R. Pierce, "Communication," in *Toward the Year 2000: Work in Progress, Daedalus*, Vol. 96 (Summer 1967), p. 921.

3. Ralph Lee Smith, *The Wired Nation*, special issue of *The Nation* (May 18, 1970), p. 605.

total system remedy called for. Ease of movement in an urban environment is not simply a product of vehicles and roadways, any more than circulation within a building depends solely on corridors and elevators. In both cases mobility depends also on how thoughtfully space has been allocated and how efficiently activities have been arranged. The great delusion is that building more capacity for movement will somehow lead to a congestion-free environment, with all the desired urban advantages.

Discovering solutions to the transportation problems of cities calls for a broader view of transportation as a subsystem of the larger system of urban living in which the origins and destinations of travel are subject to manipulation. It is in this respect that urban transport differs from interurban transport. Chicago is where it is, and so is New York, and getting from one to another requires covering a given distance. But within the city a large part of the movement is affected by a complex set of variables: population densities, the arrangement of economic activities, the condition of the environment, and the availability of housing near jobs, services, and recreation.

It is thus in our power to arrive at urban transport solutions by changing the nature of the problem. Planned communities, by rejecting the outdated concept of separating urban life into compartments by zoning, have demonstrated that the transportation problem can be contained by focusing on nontransportation solutions that emphasize accessibility rather than movement. Urban design and environment are the means of reconciling city and car and reorienting public transit. Equally significant, transportation can help to create these urban designs and environmental changes necessary to make the transport system work. In both new and redeveloped cities, conventional street systems can be transformed to space-saving patterns that make room for public parks and playgrounds, pedestrian-oriented shopping centers, the multiblock urban complex containing housing, office space, and recreation, and the new industrial estates and education parks. At the same time, the transport network can make a positive contribution to a satisfying community environment by providing the parkway, the landscaped street, the multipurpose terminal, off-street parking, tunneling, air rights development, good public transit, and nonpolluting power sources.

The extensive tooling-up for city building now going on augurs well for achieving harmony between cities and their transportation. Based on the concepts first developed in Europe and applied in selected cities around the world, communities planned for people are about to take the place of the accidental city. Motor vehicles, subways, pedestrian systems, and people movers will provide internal circulation, and expressways, high-speed ground transport, air buses, and telecommunications the interurban connections. But in the era of planned communities, these technologies will no longer dictate the kinds of cities people live in, but will help to create the communities people want. This will be accomplished by combining all the elements of city building to make possible large-scale integrated urban areas that rule out excess movement and balance transport capacity with anticipated demand.

In a world where urban population is expected to rise by one billion between now and the end of the century, new cities are obviously inevitable. The only question is whether the urban growth to come will be allowed to happen without forethought or whether it will be planned for pleasant and efficient living. Transportation capabilities provide powerful tools for rebuilding obsolete cities, moving out of the old congestion, and taking possession of the land for new patterns of urban living.

The automobile, or something like it, will continue to play a supporting role in emancipating human beings from the limited horizons and the space and time constraints that have been imposed by rural isolation. Even with major extensions of rapid transit, it now appears that half a billion vehicles may be operating on the planet before the close of the century. If we opt for unplanned cities and unbridled use of cars, the traffic jam will be absolute and the environment intolerable.

The alternative is for nations to complement economic planning with spatial planning, and for city building to be recognized as a major component of economic growth. The creation of planned urban systems and their transportation subsystems will yield many types of new cities, large and small, with varying mixtures of transportation. But the city built for urban man will maximize the ability to move while minimizing the need for unnecessary motion, and in the process will use the transport system to further the goals of the community. The basic objectives will be housing, public services, and environment that allow people to live well and not just to move better—a mobile population but also an accessible city.

TABLE A-1. *Intercity Travel in the United States, by Mode, Selected Years 1940–70*
*In billions of passenger-miles*

| Mode | 1940 | 1950 | 1960 | 1970[a] |
|---|---|---|---|---|
| Private | | | | |
| Car | 292.7 | 438.3 | 706.1 | 1,026.0 |
| Public | | | | |
| Air[b] | 1.3 | 10.1 | 34.0 | 114.0 |
| Bus | 10.2 | 22.7 | 19.3 | 25.0 |
| Rail | 24.8 | 32.5 | 21.6 | 11.0 |
| Water | 1.3 | 1.2 | 2.7 | 4.0 |
| Total public | 37.6 | 66.5 | 77.6 | 154.0 |
| *As a percentage of total[c]* | | | | |
| Private | | | | |
| Car | 88.6 | 86.8 | 90.1 | 87.0 |
| Public | | | | |
| Air[b] | 0.4 | 2.0 | 4.3 | 9.7 |
| Bus | 3.1 | 4.5 | 2.5 | 2.1 |
| Rail | 7.5 | 6.5 | 2.8 | 0.9 |
| Water | 0.4 | 0.2 | 0.3 | 0.3 |
| Total public | 11.4 | 13.2 | 9.9 | 13.1 |

Source: Transportation Association of America, *Transportation Facts and Trends*, 8th ed. (April 1971), p. 16.
a. Preliminary.
b. Includes private carriers.
c. Total public and private = 100 percent. Percentages may not add to 100 because of rounding.

TABLE A-2. *Rapid Transit Systems and Population of Major Cities of the World, 1967*

| City | Rapid transit (route-miles) | Population (millions) |
|------|-----------------------------|------------------------|
| New York | 237.4 | 7.6 |
| London | 215.0 | 10.2 |
| Paris | 104.9 | 7.6 |
| Moscow | 76.2 | 6.4 |
| Tokyo | 50.4 | 11.0 |
| West Berlin | 48.9 | 2.2 |
| Hamburg | 46.4 | 2.4 |
| Buenos Aires | 39.4 | 3.3 |
| Stockholm | 39.3 | 0.8 |
| Philadelphia | 26.1 | 2.7 |
| Boston | 23.2 | 2.5 |
| Osaka | 22.0 | 3.2 |
| Madrid | 20.7 | 2.8 |
| Toronto | 16.3 | 1.8 |
| Leningrad | 16.2 | 3.3 |
| Athens | 16.0 | 2.0 |
| Montreal | 15.9 | 1.8 |
| Cleveland | 14.8 | 1.8 |
| Milan | 8.6 | 1.7 |
| Rome | 6.8 | 2.5 |

Source: International Union of Public Transport, *Statistics of Urban Public Transport,* 2d ed. (Brussels, 1968).

TABLE A-3. *Rapid Transit and Surface Transit Patronage, Selected Cities outside the United States, 1967 and 1969*
*In millions*

| | Rapid transit passengers | | | Surface transit passengers | | |
|---|---|---|---|---|---|---|
| City | 1967 | 1969 | Per-centage change | 1967 | 1969 | Per-centage change |
| Barcelona | 211 | 197 | −7 | 376 | 327 | −13 |
| Buenos Aires | 242 | 269 | 11 | n.a. | n.a. | — |
| Hamburg | 168 | 175 | 4 | 220 | 207 | −6 |
| Lisbon | 35 | 37 | 6 | 383 | 377 | −2 |
| Madrid | 465 | 488 | 5 | 472 | 379[a] | −20 |
| Milan | 45 | 57 | 27 | 556 | 507 | −9 |
| Montreal | 146 | 126 | −14 | 267 | 287 | 7 |
| Moscow | 1,328 | 1,329 | —[b] | 1,757 | n.a. | — |
| Oslo | 20 | 26 | 30 | 99 | 68 | −31 |
| Rome | 17 | 19 | 12 | 721 | 635 | −12 |
| Rotterdam | 30 | 32 | 7 | 144 | 123 | −15 |
| Stockholm | 125 | 140 | 12 | 100 | 73 | −27 |
| Tokyo | | | | | | |
|   Teito system | 696 | 910 | 31 | 837 | 608 | −27 |
|   Municipal system | 57 | 102 | 79 | n.a. | n.a. | — |
| Toronto | 66 | 118 | 79 | n.a. | n.a. | — |

Source: Data supplied by International Union of Public Transport, Brussels, February 1970.

n.a. Not available.

a. New microbuses introduced in 1969 are not included.

b. Less than 0.1 percent.

TABLE A-4. *Transit Patronage, Selected Cities outside the United States with Surface Transit Only, 1967 and 1969*

| City | Millions of passengers | | Percentage change |
|---|---|---|---|
| | 1967 | 1969 | |
| Antwerp | 63 | 61 | −3 |
| Basel | 104 | 105 | 1 |
| Bordeaux[a] | 76 | 70 | −8 |
| Brussels | 226 | 205 | −9 |
| Geneva | 73 | 73 | 0 |
| Genoa | 235 | 188 | −20 |
| Glasgow | 384 | 324 | −16 |
| Manchester | 292 | 252 | −14 |
| Marseilles[a] | 100 | 80 | −20 |
| Melbourne | 165 | 154 | −7 |
| Prague | 573 | 572 | —[b] |
| Sydney | 232 | 220 | −5 |
| Zurich | 208 | 208 | 0 |

Source: Data supplied by International Union of Public Transport, Brussels, February 1970.

a. Fare increases may have contributed to this decline in number of riders.

b. Less than 0.1 percent.

TABLE A-5. *European and U.S. Rail Travel, 1969*

| Country | Passenger-kilometers (millions) | Passengers (millions) | Population (millions) | Per capita | |
|---|---|---|---|---|---|
| | | | | Passenger-kilometers | Number of rides |
| Austria | 6,195 | 157 | 7.4 | 837 | 21 |
| Belgium | 7,515 | 202 | 9.6 | 783 | 21 |
| Denmark | 3,291 | 116 | 4.9 | 672 | 24 |
| France | 39,140 | 607 | 50.3 | 778 | 12 |
| Germany, Federal Republic of | 36,355 | 949 | 58.7 | 619 | 16 |
| Greece | 1,435 | 12 | 8.8 | 163 | 1 |
| Italy | 29,994 | 327 | 53.2 | 564 | 6 |
| Netherlands | 7,502 | 180 | 12.9 | 582 | 14 |
| Norway | 1,564 | 29 | 3.9 | 401 | 7 |
| Spain | 12,647 | 159 | 32.9 | 384 | 5 |
| Sweden | 4,684 | 61 | 8.0 | 586 | 8 |
| Switzerland | 8,071 | 231 | 6.2 | 1,302 | 37 |
| United Kingdom | 29,612 | 805 | 55.5 | 534 | 15 |
| Yugoslavia | 10,469 | 163 | 20.4 | 513 | 8 |
| United States | 19,568 | 296 | 203.2 | 96 | 1 |

Sources: United Nations, *Annual Bulletin of Transport Statistics for Europe, 1969*, Vol. 21 (UN, 1970), Table 8; United Nations, *Statistical Yearbook, 1970* (UN, 1971), Table 18.

# Selected Readings

Advisory Commission on Intergovernmental Relations. *Urban and Rural America: Policies for Future Growth.* Washington: Government Printing Office, 1968.

*America's Changing Environment. Daedalus,* Journal of the American Academy of Arts and Sciences, Vol. 96 (Fall 1967).

Best, Robin H. *Land for New Towns: A Study of Land Use, Densities, and Agricultural Displacement.* London: Town and Country Planning Association, 1964.

Canty, Donald (ed.). *The New City.* New York: Frederick A. Praeger, 1969.

Committee for Economic Development. *Developing Metropolitan Transportation Policies: A Guide for Local Leadership.* New York: CED, 1965.

Comprehensive Planning Office, The Port of New York Authority. *Metropolitan Transportation—1980.* New York: Port of New York Authority, 1963.

Connecticut Interregional Planning Program. *Transportation,* Connecticut: Choices for Action series. State of Connecticut, 1966.

————. *Urban Development,* Connecticut: Choices for Action series. State of Connecticut, 1966.

Cowan, Peter (ed.). *Developing Patterns of Urbanization.* London: Oliver and Boyd, 1970.

Cox, Harvey G. *The Secular City: Secularization and Urbanization in Theological Perspective.* New York: Macmillan Company, 1964.

Doxiadis, Constantinos A. *Ekistics: An Introduction to the Science of Human Settlements.* London: Hutchinson Publishing Group, 1968.

Duff, Alan C. *Britain's New Towns.* London: Pall Mall Press, 1961.

Farris, Martin T., and Paul T. McElhiney. *Modern Transportation: Selected Readings.* Boston: Houghton Mifflin Company, 1967.

Gruen, Victor. *The Heart of Our Cities: The Urban Crisis, Diagnosis and Cure.* New York: Simon and Schuster, 1964.

Haworth, Lawrence. *The Good City.* Bloomington: Indiana University Press, 1963.

Jacobs, Jane. *The Death and Life of Great American Cities: The Failure of Town Planning.* New York: Random House, 1961.

Lang, A. Scheffer, and Richard M. Soberman. *Urban Rail Transit.* Cambridge: M.I.T. Press, 1963.

Lecht, Leonard A. *Goals, Priorities, and Dollars: The Next Decade.* New York: Free Press, 1966.

Lewis, John P. *Quiet Crisis in India: Economic Development and American*

*Policy.* Washington: Brookings Institution, 1962. Chapter 7: "The Role of the Town in Industrial Location."

McLuhan, Marshall. *Understanding Media: The Extensions of Man.* New York: McGraw-Hill, 1964.

Meyer, John R., John F. Kain, and Martin Wohl. *The Urban Transportation Problem.* Cambridge: Harvard University Press, 1966.

Meyerson, Martin, and others. *Face of the Metropolis.* New York: Random House, 1963.

Mumford, Lewis. *The Highway and the City.* New York: Harcourt, Brace and World, 1964.

National Council of Applied Economic Research. *Market Towns and Spatial Development in India.* New Delhi: National Council of Applied Economic Research, 1965.

Nelson, Richard R., Merton J. Peck, and Edward D. Kalachek. *Technology, Economic Growth and Public Policy.* A RAND Corporation and Brookings Institution Study. Washington: Brookings Institution, 1967.

Owen, Wilfred. *The Metropolitan Transportation Problem.* Rev. ed., Washington: Brookings Institution, 1966.

———. *Cities in the Motor Age.* New York: Viking Press, 1959; Cooper Square Publishers, 1970.

———. *Distance and Development: Transport and Communications in India.* Washington: Brookings Institution, 1968. Chapter 4: "Transport and the New Urban Geography."

Perloff, Harvey S. (ed.). *The Quality of the Urban Environment: Essays on "New Resources" in an Urban Age.* Baltimore: Johns Hopkins Press for Resources for the Future, 1969.

Perloff, Harvey S., and Lowdon Wingo, Jr. (eds.). *Issues in Urban Economics.* Baltimore: Johns Hopkins Press for Resources for the Future, 1968.

Pickard, Jerome P. *Dimensions of Metropolitanism.* Research Monograph 14. Washington: Urban Land Institute, 1967.

The President's Commission on National Goals. *Goals for Americans.* Administered by the American Assembly, Columbia University. Englewood Cliffs: Prentice-Hall, 1960.

The President's Committee on Urban Housing. *A Decent Home.* Washington: Government Printing Office, 1969.

Reports of the Steering Group and Working Group appointed by the Minister of Transport. *Traffic in Towns: A Study of the Long Term Problems of Traffic in Urban Areas.* London: Her Majesty's Stationery Office, 1963.

Rivlin, Alice M. *Systematic Thinking for Social Action.* Washington: Brookings Institution, 1971.

Rudofsky, Bernard. *Streets for People: A Primer for Americans.* New York: Doubleday and Company, 1969.

Schultze, Charles L., with Edward K. Hamilton and Allen Schick. *Setting National Priorities: The 1971 Budget.* Washington: Brookings Institution, 1970.

Schultze, Charles L., Edward R. Fried, Alice M. Rivlin, and Nancy H. Teeters. *Setting National Priorities: The 1972 Budget.* Washington: Brookings Institution, 1971.

Smerk, George M. *Urban Transportation: The Federal Role.* Bloomington: Indiana University Press, 1965.

——— (ed.). *Readings in Urban Transportation.* Bloomington: Indiana University Press, 1968.

Thompson, Wilbur R. *A Preface to Urban Economics.* Baltimore: Johns Hopkins Press for Resources for the Future, 1965.

*Toward the Year 2000: Work in Progress. Daedalus,* Journal of the American Academy of Arts and Sciences, Vol. 96 (Summer 1967).

U.S. Congress, House. Committee on Science and Astronautics. *Science and Technology and the Cities.* A Compilation of Papers Prepared for the Tenth Meeting of the Panel on Science and Technology. Washington: Government Printing Office, 1969.

Whyte, William H. *The Last Landscape.* New York: Doubleday and Company, 1968.